COMMUNITY

THE NEW TESTAMENT CHURCH—THE ESSENCE
OF FELLOWSHIP

ADAM ROBINSON

**youth
specialties**

Community: The New Testament Church—The Essence of Fellowship
Copyright 2008 Clarity Publishers, Inc.

Youth Specialties resources, 300 S. Pierce St., El Cajon, CA 92020 are published by Zondervan, 5300 Patterson Ave. SE, Grand Rapids, MI 49530.

ISBN 978-0-310-27907-5

Published in association with Yates & Yates, LLP, Attorneys and Counselors, Orange, California

Cover design by Brandi K. Etheredge
Interior design by SharpSeven Design

Printed in the United States of America

08 09 10 11 12 • 20 19 18 17 16 15 14 13 12 11 10 9 8 7 6 5 4 3 2 1

CONTENTS

INTRO

HOW TO USE THIS BOOK

The purpose of this 48-week journal is to help you learn the story of the New Testament church. Although the events surrounding the formation of the church happened nearly 2,000 years ago, they're still relevant today, and you can apply biblical truths to your life as a twenty-first–century Christian. Through this journal you'll learn about being a member of your church, as well as a member of the global Church that's made up of all the Christians in the world. This journal includes a few sections to help you as you learn. Here's how to use them:

Introductions: These are short sections that introduce each week of devotionals. Read the Introduction section to get a picture of what the week's devotions will center on.

Daily Devotions: Now we're getting to the good stuff. This journal is designed to walk you through five days of devotions each week. And each devotion contains a Scripture passage and a paragraph of text. Always start by reading the Scripture passage in your Bible, and then read the text. Look for ways that the text unlocks some truths of Scripture you may not have noticed before.

Daily Questions: After each devotional paragraph, you'll find questions designed to get you thinking. When you read these questions, take a moment to really consider what they're asking. Listen to the Holy Spirit as he teaches you through Scripture. Then record your thoughts in the Journal Space.

Journal Spaces: You'll notice this book is different from many books you've read before because it's designed to be filled with your thoughts. Use the space provided to record your reactions to each devotional passage. Or use it to write a prayer request or praise to God. Use it any way you please. It's your journal. There are no rules, just guidelines. The important thing is to listen to God and open your heart in response to his leading.

If you take the time to read the devotionals prayerfully and with the anticipation that God will reveal new things to you, then you'll be amazed at what will flow through your pen or pencil and onto the pages.

NOW WHAT?

It was a pretty amazing time to be a disciple. Jesus had been crucified and raised from the dead. And in the beginning of Acts, we find Jesus and the disciples hanging out together. He'd already told them to wait in Jerusalem for the Holy Spirit to come upon them, but this confused the disciples. So, logically, they asked Jesus about it. Jesus calmly explained to them that it wasn't their place to know his plan; they'd know when it happened. And no sooner had the words left his mouth when, all of a sudden—he was gone. Ascended. Whisked away in the clouds. Wow—imagine that!

After three years of healings, preaching, and traveling, Jesus had been murdered, had risen from the grave, and had ascended into heaven. Then there they were—11 guys standing on a hillside, staring into the sky with one question in their minds...

Now what?

This is how the book of Acts begins. More importantly, this is how the Church began. And by Church (capital C), I mean all the believers in Jesus Christ around the world. The same local church that you're now a part of in a sense originated 2,000 years ago by those 11 guys. When Jesus ascended back into heaven, it wasn't the end of the story. It was a whole new beginning. These guys thought they'd seen it all. But in God's eyes, they'd barely begun.

Maybe that's your story, too. Maybe you believe you've seen it all. You're saved. You believe in God; you believe in his Son, Jesus; and you go to church like you're supposed to. But what do you do now? What comes after being saved? How are you supposed to grow in your faith? That's where the Church comes in.

God isn't interested only in making sure you're saved. That's the beginning, but there's much more in store for you. God has a plan for your life, but it's not for you only—it's for all of us. You may not know it, but when you became a son or daughter of God, you didn't get adopted by the heavenly Father only. You were also adopted by a whole family of brothers and sisters. That family is the Church.

We're going to look at one of the most important aspects of our spiritual lives. In fact, it's so important that your spiritual walk will never really work without it. What is it? Community. I know it sounds kind of dry. But once you get a taste of it, you'll wonder how you ever lived without it. Community isn't just going to church or wearing a Christian T-shirt or showing up for church events. It's much, much more.

Imagine the relationship you have with your best friends. You talk, you hang out, you like them. If they were in trouble, then you'd help them out—no questions asked. If you were in trouble, then you know they'd be there in a minute. And you probably tell them more about yourself than you tell other people. Why? Because you're connected in a way you can't really put into words. It's different from your relationships with everyone else.

Now imagine having that kind of relationship with 10 people. With 50. With 500. Of course you couldn't spend as much time with each person, but imagine knowing that all of those people would be there for you in a heartbeat. Imagine loving that many people and being willing to help them no matter what. Imagine not having to wear a mask in front of all those people because they all love you just the way you are. And every single one of them serves God and helps you to do the same. Now you're starting to see it: The kingdom of God.

God's community.

The New Testament church was just like that. What began as a disjointed, ragtag group of unschooled men became the foundation for a force of change that would eventually touch all parts of the globe. The New Testament church is your spiritual heritage. And although the events surrounding its formation took place almost 2,000 years ago, we can still learn so much today. It's an incredible story!

We're going to examine how to build real community. We'll walk through the book of Acts and see how it all began. We'll learn how to create that same kind of community right where we are. It's a huge task, but it's one that will shape everything about you and me and all of us—together.

So you may be asking yourself, *Now what?*

Well, turn the page and find out...

WEEK 1
GOD'S ARMY: WHAT IS THE CHURCH?

MEMORY VERSE

"The stone the builders rejected has become the capstone; the Lord has done this, and it is marvelous in our eyes." (Psalm 118:22-23)

INTRODUCTION

It started quietly enough. Off in a corner, Jesus asked a simple question of his trusted friends. Peter answered for all of them: We believe you're the Son of the living God. They had little understanding of the meaning of that one simple statement. That confession was the foundation of a world-shattering new reality: God was present among them and was creating something that would change the world for all time. That reality is the Church of Jesus Christ.

Today you and I are the latest in an unbroken line of believers that started way back then. And what started on that day wasn't a movement, a cult, or a philosophy. Instead, God decided to build a family—a living, breathing family of millions—all linked through God's Holy Spirit. If you're a Christian, then it's your family. God sent Jesus to be the head of a new nation of people, a nation without physical borders, racial divisions, or social barriers.

Welcome to the citizenship of the Spirit. Today all believers across the world form the Church, and small parts of that larger body meet together as local churches just like yours. This week we'll try to answer the question, "What is the Church?" and find out how we fit in. We'll discover that God has plans not just for you, but for all of us—together.

DAILY DEVOTIONS

Day 1
Matthew 16:13-20

In Jesus' day, everyone was confused about who he was, and no one fully grasped his mission as the Messiah. Living on this side of history, we're better able to understand his mission; we know the end of the story. But lots of people are still confused about Jesus today. Some believe he's just a teacher, others believe he's one of many pathways to heaven, and still others believe he's a lunatic. And then some people don't believe he existed at all.

Before we can be a part of the Church, we have to answer this question for ourselves: *Do I really believe that Jesus is the Son of God and that he can save me from my sins?*

The only way into the Church is to confess Jesus as Lord. Have you done that?

If no one you knew believed in Jesus, would you? Why?

If everyone you knew decided that Jesus wasn't really the Son of God, would you? Why?

Day 2
Mark 10:17-31

This is one of those classic moments in Scripture—the moment in which someone decides to leave everything and follow Christ. But put yourself in Peter's shoes. He'd already said yes and left his home and his job. He was able to do what the rich young ruler wasn't. Jesus told Peter he'd receive a hundredfold of what he'd left behind "in this present age." So how does that work? Peter wasn't the father of hundreds by the time he died. Jesus was trying to help us understand that when you join him, you join his family. Through Christ we become connected to all other believers. So instead of being out on your own, all of us in the Church support and love one another. You already have lots of fathers, mothers, brothers, and sisters just because you're part of your church. Welcome to the family!

Have you made the kind of choice that Peter did?

How are you building relationships with the people in your church?

Day 3
1 Corinthians 12:27-31; Colossians 1:18

Being a part of a family means different things as you grow up. At first you just have the family's name; but as you grow, you take on more responsibilities. However, you never lose the name. In these passages

Paul told us a lot about who we are as a Church. First, in Colossians 1:18 he let us know who's the boss: Jesus is the Head of the Church. Not a pastor or a group of men—only Jesus himself. Yet in the 1 Corinthians passage, Paul reveals that inside of that Church every one of us has a role to play, just like every part of your body has a specific function. So while Jesus functions as the authority of the Church, as well as the glue that holds it all together, you also have a unique role to fill that no one else can. Without you, the Church won't work the way Jesus wants it to. And that makes you indispensable.

How can you honor Jesus today as the Head of his Church?

Do you know what your role in the Church is? Ask Christ to show you.

Day 4
1 Peter 2:9-10

Do you know your heritage? Perhaps there are Native Americans in your lineage—or you may have Scottish blood. Knowing you're part of a larger family gives you a sense of place in the history of the world, letting you know you're not just the new kid on the block. You may not know your human heritage, but you can know your spiritual heritage. Peter, a Jew, reminded all the believers in his church—regardless of their race—that because they belonged to Christ, they were a part of God's people and members of God's kingdom. This is your spiritual heritage. Being a Christian isn't just about knowing Jesus. It's about being a part of what God is doing in all of us all over the world.

How does it feel to know you're a part of a larger spiritual kingdom?

How should this knowledge change the way you live as a believer?

Day 5
Ephesians 5:25-32

You're probably not married, but follow me on this one. Paul is trying to show us what being the Church is like, and he uses marriage as the example. Jesus is the groom and the Church is the bride. Notice that you alone aren't the bride, but all Christians together. God is preparing all of us that we might be God's spotless bride. Reread the passage and look at how Jesus cares for his Church. God cares tremendously about the health of your church.

Your church may be experiencing some problems, but God is in the process of making all of us pure, holy, and unified. How is Jesus doing this in the life of your church?

How should we as the Church respond to Christ as the groom?

If this is how God cares for his Church, then how should we treat the other members of our local church?

WEEK 2
THE POWER OF THE SPIRIT: JESUS' ASCENSION AND THE HOLY SPIRIT

MEMORY VERSE

"'But you will receive power when the Holy Spirit comes on you; and you will be my witnesses in Jerusalem, and in all Judea and Samaria, and to the ends of the earth.'" (Acts 1:8)

INTRODUCTION

Graduation Day! Can you imagine how great it's going to feel to be done with school, be more in charge of your own schedule, and be allowed to enjoy your freedom? But then again, it's kind of comfortable where you are. You have a schedule, life is predictable, you know everyone, and you know where everything is. Do you really have to leave all that behind?

In Acts 1:4-14 the disciples were struggling to make that same kind of transition. They'd gotten used to having Jesus around, and they were probably thrilled about this promised Holy Spirit. But I'll bet they secretly wished things could just stay the same. Couldn't Jesus hang around a little longer? But in order to achieve his plan for the spread of the gospel, Jesus had to leave his friends. He wanted them to experience the fullness of a relationship with him and to have the power to spread the Word throughout the region and the world. For that they'd need the Holy Spirit.

This week we're going to look at what Jesus had to say about the Holy Spirit and how he works in our lives. He's our intimate link to the Father, and everything we need is found in him. The Holy Spirit that was promised to the disciples is the same Holy Spirit that lives in each of us, so it's important that we know how to live in him.

Get ready, because the Spirit may be more than you bargained for.

DAILY DEVOTIONS

Day 1
Acts 1:4-14

I don't like to wait, and I'm sure the disciples didn't either. Can you imagine waiting for this promise to be fulfilled? I wonder what they expected. Whatever they thought was coming, one thing they knew for sure: It would be powerful.

When the Holy Spirit came upon them, the disciples had power to accomplish whatever God asked of them. This is important for us to remember, too. God isn't asking us to just give him our best shot at ministering to others. God sends his Spirit to help us accomplish every task God assigns. Our job is to rely on God for all of our needs and stop trying to accomplish life on our own. It's hard to give up control, but the results will prove that it's well worth it.

Do you truly believe God will empower you through the Spirit to accomplish anything?

How are you relying on God's Spirit to live the Christian life today?

Day 2
John 16:5-11

Jesus knew how the disciples would feel without him around. So he explained to them how the Spirit would work in their lives. Even though Jesus wouldn't be around physically, the Spirit would continue to do all the things Jesus had done. And because the Spirit would be inside all believers, that ministry took on a much larger scale. Jesus would still be doing his Father's work; he'd just do it through the Holy Spirit. Even now Jesus is doing the Father's work through the Holy Spirit inside you. So in effect, Jesus didn't leave. Jesus placed his Spirit in us, not just the first-century disciples, so we can all join him in his work.

Do you believe God can use you to accomplish his will? Do you believe he will?

Ask God to use you to advance the kingdom today.

Day 3
John 16:12-15

The disciples had gotten used to the luxury of having Jesus around. When they had a question, they could simply ask him. But what would happen after his ascension? Jesus told them the Spirit would continue to speak to them and help them understand everything they needed to know. Far from being silent, the Holy Spirit would be their constant guide to point them to truth. Now we can have the same privilege the disciples had and talk to God whenever we want. The Spirit isn't just for full-time church staff; he dwells in every believer. So if you've become a Christian, then this privilege is for you. The question for us is this: Are we listening?

Have you ever listened for the voice of the Holy Spirit in your life? How did you know it was the Spirit?

Ask the Father to make the voice of the Holy Spirit very clear in your life.

Day 4
John 14:25-27

So how do you hear the voice of the Holy Spirit? What exactly does the Spirit sound like? It will take some time to recognize it, but the clearest way to know if you're hearing from God is to listen for him in Scripture. Here Jesus told us the Holy Spirit would remind us of all the things Jesus said. We find those things revealed in God's Word. So when you're in a situation and suddenly Scripture comes to mind, you're most likely hearing the Holy Spirit. But in order for the Spirit to remind us of Scripture, we have to know Scripture.

Reading our Bibles every day puts us in a great place to make sure we'll hear from the Holy Spirit. Do you read your Bible every day?

Has God ever spoken to you by reminding you of Scripture?

Ask God to remind you of things he wants you to know today.

Day 5
Acts 1:8

Have you ever been given a job that seemed too much for you? That's probably how the disciples felt after hearing Jesus say this. They'd just been given the job of telling the whole world about Jesus. (Hey, no pressure, right?) But Jesus, through the Spirit, was going to help them go tell others about him. Do you realize this verse is directed toward you as well? God has given you the Spirit, and now he wants you to do what the disciples did: Tell others about your faith. Have you ever done that? Are you scared to do it? The disciples were scared, too, but they still did it. And the Spirit really helped them.

Pray that you'll have the opportunity to talk to someone about Jesus today. You might be surprised by what happens.

WEEK 3
THE CHURCH FOUNDERS: THE CHOOSING OF MATTHIAS

MEMORY VERSE

"It was he who gave some to be apostles, some to be prophets, some to be evangelists, and some to be pastors and teachers, to prepare God's people for works of service, so that the body of Christ may be built up." (Ephesians 4:11-12)

INTRODUCTION

Every story has a beginning, and yours goes all the way back to the disciples. One disciple in particular, Peter, is a big figure in the Church. He's depicted in paintings, he wrote a couple of books in the New Testament, and it's said he has this sweet gig at the pearly gates. But back in the book of Acts, none of this was on his radar. In fact, all the disciples were a little confused. Jesus had always made the decisions, but suddenly the disciples—a group of ordinary Joes—were alone. They must have thought, *We're here, but what are we supposed to do?*

They went to work anyway, starting with the decision to replace Judas. Jesus had selected 12 disciples; therefore, it seemed important to continue to have 12. The disciples prayed that God would show them the right person, and God did. Matthias was chosen to replace Judas.

From there it's all history. Everything was happening according to God's plan. Little did the disciples know they were the beginning of the Church of Jesus Christ. The church you attend today can be traced back to these original followers of Christ.

This week we're looking at the apostles, the people Paul referred to as the foundation of the Church. As we study them, try to put yourself in their shoes. Think about what it would've been like to see the early Church get started. Imagine how people might have treated them. Try to picture the kind of faith the apostles must have had.

DAILY DEVOTIONS

Day 1
Acts 1:15-26

Scripture doesn't record anything about Matthias outside of today's passage. But even in these few verses we find out a lot. We know Matthias had been traveling with Jesus from the beginning. He was an eyewitness to Jesus' ministry, death, and resurrection.

Would you have stuck with Jesus even if you hadn't been one of the chosen few? Matthias wasn't part of the 12 that Jesus originally picked, but he followed Jesus anyway. That says a lot. Remember, this was before Pentecost; the Holy Spirit hadn't arrived yet. Matthias was signing on to an almost certain death. These are the kind of people God built the Church upon.

If Jesus gave you a chance to serve today, would you do it?

Will you follow Jesus no matter where he calls you?

Day 2
2 Peter 1:16-19

Recently I met the general and the photographer who fought in the Battle of Ia Drang at the beginning of the Vietnam War. This battle was depicted in the movie *We Were Soldiers*. But as I talked with these veterans, the movie wasn't just a movie to me anymore; it was real life. Everything I heard was more dramatic because I knew these guys were actually there.

In this passage Peter reminds his readers that *he was there*. Everything they believed could be trusted because Peter is an eyewitness. What we believe isn't just a philosophy concocted by religious leaders; it's the truth. Peter wanted the believers to know they could trust the Scripture. And Peter believed because he'd seen things with his own eyes.

What are some of your experiences with Christ that remind you he's real?

Do you ever doubt the Scripture or choose not to believe?

How does this passage help you deal with those doubts?

Day 3
Ephesians 2:19-22

You may not think about it or even realize it, but you're a part of a long heritage of faith. The church you're now a part of didn't start with your parents, or even their parents, or those gray-haired folks in your church. No, you and I are part of a spiritual lineage that goes back about 2,000 years to Peter, John, and all the other disciples. It's a rich history, one that finds its roots in Jesus Christ. There aren't any apostles alive today, nor will there be in the future. But Paul says their teaching is the foundation of our faith, a foundation that Jesus crafted. Think about all the famous believers throughout history: the apostles, St. Augustine, Martin Luther, Billy Graham. Do you realize you're part of the same family tree they are?

How does it feel to be in the same spiritual lineage as well-known Christians throughout history?

How is Jesus changing your life as he changed theirs?

Day 4
Revelation 1:9-11

John is the brother of James and one of the inner three disciples (along with Peter and James) with whom Jesus shared the most. According to tradition he's the only apostle who did not die a martyr's death. The passage you read today was most likely written around AD 95. By this time John was about 90 years old and had been serving Christ for more than 60 years. He'd watched almost all of his friends die, and at this point he's exiled alone on an island for his faith. But look at what John is doing: He's having his own worship service. His devotion is such that nothing—not death, not torture, not long periods of suffering—could shake his faith. Why? Because he knew Jesus.

How does your relationship with Jesus help you deal with hard times?

Ask Jesus to help you stand firm when things seem too much to bear.

Day 5
Acts 4:32-35

This passage gives a small glimpse of what the early Church looked like. It's a small glimpse because while the early Church faced lots of hard times, the period in this passage depicts a body of believers running on all cylinders, full steam ahead. Can you imagine what your church would look like if, as described in this passage, everyone was of one heart and one mind? If your leaders boldly and powerfully proclaimed Jesus' resurrection at all times? If everyone freely shared everything they owned (even their land, and homes, and money) as if they had no claim on any of it? And no one was ever in need because those with much always gave to those with little or nothing?

This can be your church! Why? Because today's Christians are powered by the same Holy Spirit who gave strength to the believers of the early Church.

What can you do to get the ball rolling? Then how can you help others get on board to make your church look a little bit more like the one described in Acts 4?

Ask God right now for the vision and passion to make your church—or for starters, your youth group!—the kind of "body" that turns heads and gets people excited about God.

WEEK 4
BAPTISM OF THE SPIRIT: THE HOLY SPIRIT AT PENTECOST

MEMORY VERSE

"Do you not know that your body is a temple of the Holy Spirit, who is in you, whom you have received from God? You are not your own; you were bought at a price. Therefore honor God with your body." (1 Corinthians 6:19-20)

INTRODUCTION

It was dramatic. Rushing wind...pyrotechnics...crowds reeling in amazement...and one of the most effective sermons ever preached. This is how the Church was born at Pentecost. In one day more than 3,000 people began the church in Jerusalem.

Those believers were the start of something big. Since then the Church has faithfully passed the message of Jesus Christ from generation to generation throughout the ages. Eventually someone told you. The church you're now a part of grew from the message of Christ that the early Christians presented thousands of years ago.

The Holy Spirit of God made a surprise entrance at Pentecost, assuring us that from then on we'd be able to do things that used to be impossible. The Spirit now empowers us, guides us to the truth, teaches us, and helps us share our faith. With the Spirit, amazing things are suddenly a possibility.

As believers, one of our main tasks is to remain connected to the Holy Spirit. This week we'll look at how the Spirit helps us and find out how to take advantage of the many miraculous opportunities the Spirit gives us every day.

DAILY DEVOTIONS

Day 1
Acts 2:1-4; Ephesians 1:13-14

I don't know about you, but I've never seen tongues of fire. Ever. On anyone. So how do we know we have the Spirit in our lives? The disciples got this grand miracle, but what about us? Paul tells us in Ephesians that we receive the Spirit when we first believe in Jesus Christ and become Christians. You have the Spirit right now. And even though you may not have seen a grand miracle like the apostles did when they received the Spirit, that same Spirit is in you. The Spirit empowered the early disciples, and he will do that for us as well. The real question is will we rely on the Spirit?

Think back on some of the moments in which you knew the Spirit was working in your life. How can we stay in touch with the Spirit on a continual basis?

Are you doing those things?

Day 2
Ephesians 5:18

This is one of those verses that can be a little confusing. Don't we already have the Spirit? Then why do we need to be filled again? Did the Spirit leave? Absolutely not! Paul knew that all believers have the Holy Spirit dwelling in them, but Paul also knew that not all believers *rely* on the Holy Spirit all the time. While the Spirit is always with us, we choose every day whether or not we want the Spirit to be in control. We can be filled with ourselves, or we can be led by the Spirit. Paul reminded us to choose to be filled with God's Spirit each day, rather than just doing our best on our own.

Would you describe your life as being filled with the Spirit? Why or why not?

Ask God to help you empty yourself and be filled with the Spirit today.

Day 3
Ephesians 3:14-21

This was Paul's prayer for the Ephesians, and I'd be willing to say it's also God's desire for us. Read it through a few times. (No, really—read it again.)
What are some of the things Paul wants to happen to us? In verse 16 Paul says the Spirit will strengthen your soul. Verse 17 tells us why: So we can have a deeper walk with Jesus. Verse 18 says we'll have power when we dwell on the amazing love God has for us. In verse 19 Paul says that if this happens, then we can be filled completely with God's power. This is a pretty amazing prayer. And all of this is for you. Why don't you pray this for your life?

Ask God to do the things for you that are mentioned in today's Scripture passage.

Pray this prayer for your friends, family, and church as well.

Day 4
Ephesians 6:18-20

Why did Paul ask for prayer? Isn't he, you know, Paul? Super-Christian Paul? Paul knew the Spirit wasn't just in him but in all his Christian friends as well. He also knew that God is doing something in all of us—together. This means Paul couldn't be a loner; he needed the help of others. So when you face problems, it's important to ask for help—not just from God but also from God's people. Why? Because God's Spirit is inside all of us. That's why Paul could ask the Ephesians to pray "in the Spirit." Your prayers for others and theirs for you are incredibly powerful. Paul needed those prayers, and we need our friends' prayers as well.

Do you ever ask people to pray for you?

Do you ever pray for others?

Do you really believe prayer will accomplish anything?

Day 5
Acts 4:3-12

Probably no one in this story was as surprised as Peter. Remember, this is the same person who talked boldly about following Christ to his death but then denied Jesus only hours later. Not the picture of the most effective follower. But look at Peter in today's Scripture passage. He is bold, he's preaching, he isn't afraid of being thrown in jail. Something is different—but what? The presence of the Holy Spirit is what changed Peter. Yes, he still made mistakes; but he had the power to stay faithful because he was relying on the Holy Spirit, not on himself. See the difference between Spirit-led living and just trying to do your best?

When you're challenged or tempted, do you turn to God for help?

Do you really believe the Holy Spirit will empower you?

Ask God to make the power of the Holy Spirit very real and present in your life.

WEEK 5
THE CHURCH'S MESSAGE: PETER SPEAKS

MEMORY VERSE

"God has raised this Jesus to life, and we are all witnesses of the fact."
(Acts 2:32)

INTRODUCTION

"Man Raised from the Dead!" It sounds like a headline you'd read in the *National Enquirer*. But this fact is the basis for Christianity. The heart of the gospel isn't a list of rules or regulations. It's Jesus' message that we need—and can have—new life. And this new life is available to anyone who believes Jesus died and arose from the dead.

In Acts 2:14-33 Peter follows up the incredible baptism of the Holy Spirit with an awesome Pentecost sermon. He speaks the truth about the Holy Spirit—that God had promised it and kept that promise. And then Peter boldly proclaims that the Jesus they'd all watched die is alive again. More than anything else, this defined the beliefs of the apostles and the early Church. Without the resurrection there is no Christianity because Christ would still be dead.

The truths about Jesus in Peter's sermon have always been the Church's central message; it should be a message we claim for ourselves. Because Jesus is alive, we can have a relationship with him and know he's working in our lives on a daily basis. It gives us confidence in the hope that one day we, too, will be resurrected. This week we'll look at what the resurrection means to us on a daily basis.

DAILY DEVOTIONS

Day 1
Luke 24:36-48

It's time for a reality check. Do you actually believe Jesus rose from the dead? Think about this truth—not just a story or a sermon illustration: Jesus actually died on a Friday, and and on Sunday morning he walked out of a tomb. This is the message of the Church—that Jesus is alive today because he actually rose from the grave. But it makes no difference in your life unless you believe it yourself. If you have questions about this, then ask a parent or a youth leader. But figure it out, no matter what it costs you. Even the disciples needed a little convincing. Jesus wants you to have a faith of your own.

Ask God to show you the truth and help you believe and understand it.

Day 2
Colossians 1:9-12

Have you ever felt as if your prayers are bouncing off the ceiling—as if no one is really listening? Some people believe we're stupid for praying to an invisible God. But the resurrection changes things. We don't pray to a dead god. Our God rose from the dead and is alive today. That means we can have a real relationship with him. Knowing and obeying him isn't just about rules; it's about getting to know him personally. The word *knowledge* in these verses means having an experience with someone, not just knowing facts about the person. Jesus is alive and seeking a real relationship with you. Are you doing the same with him?

Check your prayers. Do you pray as if someone is really listening and might talk back?

Are you building a real relationship with Jesus?

Day 3
2 Corinthians 5:17

This is one of those verses to memorize. Make sure you underline it in your Bible. Think about it for a minute: When Jesus rose from the dead, he had a brand-new life. He wasn't a mutilated man anymore; he received a new body and a new life. When you became a Christian, that's what happened to you, too. You may look the same on the outside, but something cataclysmic has happened in your soul. You're a new creation. You'll see Jesus face to face one day. And you have the power of God inside you. You didn't join a club or decide to live differently. When you became a Christian, you became a true child of God. Wow! What a change!

Dwell on this verse throughout the day and think about what it really means.

Day 4
Ephesians 1:17-21

Sometimes I feel as if it's impossible to live the kind of Christian life I should.

Following God is just really hard sometimes. But look at what Paul said here. He said the same power that God used to raise Jesus from the dead is working in us right now. The same power. The resurrection is the greatest miracle of all time, and that's the kind of power God is using in our lives. Our power doesn't always work, but God's power always succeeds. No matter who you are, if you're in Christ, then that same power is working in you.

Are there any places in your life where you're relying on your own strength instead of God's?

Choose to actively rely on God's power instead.

Day 5
Romans 6:4

Many times I hear believers hurling insults at non-Christians because of their sinful behavior. But that wasn't the message of the early Christians. And while Paul didn't tolerate sin, he knew that his only hope began and ended with a new life in Jesus. The Savior was alive, and Paul and other early Church leaders preached the message of new life in him. The same is true for us: Before we can talk about others' behavior, we have to talk about new life. Without that power no one will see Jesus in us.

When we talk about Jesus, do we rely on his power?

When you share your faith, do you talk more about the rules and guidelines of what Christians should or shouldn't do—or do you talk about a relationship with God?

Is your life more about rules or a relationship with God through Jesus?

WEEK 6
SILVER OR GOLD I DO NOT HAVE: HEALING OF THE BEAUTIFUL BEGGAR

MEMORY VERSE

"And let us consider how we may spur one another on toward love and good deeds. Let us not give up meeting together, as some are in the habit of doing, but let us encourage one another—and all the more as you see the Day approaching." (Hebrews 10:24-25)

INTRODUCTION

You've seen the signs: CAUTION! MEN AT WORK. SPEEDING FINES DOUBLE WHEN WORKERS PRESENT. Orange signs, cones, and barricades—these are the everyday things that let us know what's ahead.

Did you know God is always working? There are no flares or flashing lights that call us to look. We have to be sensitive to the opportunities around us. We have to sense God's Spirit moving in us. We have to learn to be aware, to be alive to the possibilities.

Peter and John sensed an opportunity one afternoon while they were on their way to pray. They saw a man who needed new legs. They saw a man who needed a handout to get his meal for the day. But they saw something more. They saw a man who needed Jesus. They knew from their own experience that if they could introduce this beggar to Christ, then he'd have all he really needed.

This week we're going to be challenged to see where God is at work and join God.

DAILY DEVOTIONS

Day 1
Acts 3:1-7

What do you see when you look at people? Peter and John were on their way to worship when they were met with human need. They didn't turn their heads; they didn't hurry by. Instead, they looked and saw the beggar's heart. He needed more than money. He needed more than healing. He needed Jesus Christ. How many times do we look to the wrong things to provide what we need? Money, education, health, popularity, and power are empty compared to a genuine relationship with Jesus Christ. The passage challenges us to look around to see the needs of people and to meet those needs with the good news of Jesus.

What are the real needs within your circle of friends?

Where are your friends looking to find fulfillment?

Ask God for the opportunity to give someone a relationship with Jesus this week.

Day 2
Acts 3:6-10

What do people see when they look at you? We never learn this man's real name, but everyone knew him as the cripple who sat at the temple gate called Beautiful. Then he was healed by the name of Jesus Christ, and he began to praise God. He couldn't help but share and show the difference Jesus had made in his life. The majority of us don't have newly healed feet and ankles, but we do have lives that have been transformed by God's Spirit at work in us. The beggar from the Beautiful gate shows us how we can declare the glory of God with what we do and with what we say, so people can look at our lives and be filled with wonder over what Christ has done.

How do you act differently because of your relationship with Jesus?

In what ways are you verbally expressing your faith?

Thank God for the changes he's made in you and ask for the courage to declare it to the world.

Day 3
2 Timothy 2:22

Have you ever read a passage and said to yourself, *I can't do that!* Let's be honest: Some things that are easy to do during your quiet time get a lot harder to do when you walk out your door. Look at Paul's advice. I'm sure you're not shocked by the call to run away from evil, youthful desires. But read the rest of the verse. God doesn't expect us to tackle this life alone. Our Father provides godly people to help us along. You need Christian friends to help you through, and they need you.

Do you have these kinds of friends?

Are you looking for them?

Think about the things this passage asks us to do. Pray today about how you and your believing friends could do them together.

Day 4
Colossians 3:15-17

Verse 17 in today's passage is one of those verses I always thought I understood. It sounds pretty straightforward, doesn't it? Just do everything for God. But in the original language (Greek), the word *you* is plural. In fact, every time you see the word *you* in this passage, it's not talking about you alone. It's referring to the whole Church. Now that changes things entirely. I'm not expected to walk with God by myself; I'm supposed to do it with other people. I need them, and they need me. That's why verses 15 and 16 read as they do.

Are you talking to others about what you read in the Bible?

Do you have friendships in which that kind of conversation happens naturally?

Who are some people you can work with to follow Christ? Pray that God will strengthen your friendships today.

Day 5
1 Corinthians 5:9-11

Paul gives us some useful guidance in this passage. There have been lots of believers who don't want to have anything to do with non-Christians. Many Christians hang out only with other Christians, and as a result they've forgotten how to get along with the rest of the world. But, as Paul states here, Jesus never intended for us to do that. Paul has strong words for those who claim to be Christians but act like the world. He says that if people don't act like believers, then they shouldn't be treated like believers. God is building a real family among us, but we cannot condone the actions of people who say one thing and do another. The goal isn't to condemn hypocrites but to help them see they can't have it both ways. You have to choose which family you want to belong to and then act accordingly.

Is there someone you need to confront in love about her behavior?

Pray that God will give you wisdom and love to challenge your friend.

WEEK 7
PHYSICAL OPPOSITION: PETER, JOHN, AND THE SANHEDRIN

MEMORY VERSE

"But we are not of those who shrink back and are destroyed, but of those who believe and are saved." (Hebrews 10:39)

INTRODUCTION

At the entrance to the Colosseum in Rome stands a huge iron cross. It was erected to commemorate the countless number of Christians who were killed for sport in that place and throughout the Roman Empire. Scary as it may seem, throughout history people have given their lives just for claiming to be Christians and refusing to deny Jesus. And while the Colosseum may seem millions of miles away from your daily life, persecution and death are a present-day reality for many Christians around the world today.

Peter and John knew this kind of persecution. In Acts 4:1-12 they were thrown in jail just because they were preaching the gospel. And that was just the beginning.

Our lives may never be at risk simply because we're Christians. But one of the things we'll have to deal with is opposition. Jesus said that since people hated him, they'd also hate us for no other reason than because we love God. It seems odd, but it happens.

You've probably already experienced people excluding you or making fun of you just for your beliefs. This week we're going to look at some responses to physical threats and how we can best use these situations to be witnesses for Christ.

DAILY DEVOTIONS

Day 1
Acts 4:1-12

No one said this was going to be easy. Peter and John got a taste of what was to come as the religious leaders got together and told them to shut up—or else. It had to be intimidating for Peter and John to stare down these men who were more educated than them and tell them they were missing the point. But even though they were threatened, Peter and John wouldn't back down. People will pressure you—verbally, silently, or even physically—to be quiet about Christ. During times like that, you can't rely on your own power; you have to rely on God's power to give you courage and strength to stand firm. See how Peter relies on the Spirit in verse 8?

How do you respond when people try to intimidate you? Do you rely on Christ for your response?

Ask God to give you courage to stand firm when things get tough.

Day 2
Acts 5:17-42

They did what? How could anyone be excited about being flogged? Flogging, by the way, is not like a spanking. It's extremely brutal and painful. So why were they rejoicing? Jesus had warned them this would happen—that they'd follow in his footsteps and be physically persecuted. So when they were beaten as Jesus was, and for the same reasons, they knew they were on the right track. They had a joy that was more important than the pain. They didn't go looking for a beating, but they endured it because Jesus had done the same thing. It's never fun to deal with persecution, but we can rejoice that we're walking in Jesus' footsteps when it happens.

Why is it hard to offer praise in the midst of suffering?

What can you focus on if you find yourself in a similar situation?

Day 3
Acts 16:22-30

Here's another story of people being happy after a beating. Look at how Paul responds. After Paul and Silas prayed, God sent a miraculous earthquake to set them free. But when the cell doors opened, Paul and Silas stayed put. What was the deal? Well, look at the result. Paul could have thought about himself and walked out with his head held high, saying, "See what my God can do?" But instead he thought about the jailer (who got saved—along with his whole family).

When there's an opportunity to show his love for people, Jesus never lets it escape. When you're physically intimidated or hurt for the name of Christ, it's very natural to think about just yourself. Paul knew God could use his beating to save someone else. This in no way means God wants those things to happen to you, but we have to look at the bigger picture when things like this occur.

Why did Paul have such little regard for himself?

Ask God to show you how good can come out of some seemingly bad situations in your life.

Day 4
Revelation 5:9-11

Stephen is recorded as the first martyr of the Christian church. The word *martyr* literally means "witness." Believers who are killed serve as witnesses to a sinful world that Christ is real. You may not hear a lot about martyrs today, but believers all over the world risk their lives daily by proclaiming to be Christians. Believe it or not, there were more Christians martyred during the 20th century than in all other centuries combined. And it's happening right now, too. At this very moment, Christians are being persecuted just like the disciples were in the book of Acts.

Take some time today to remember those who are giving their lives for the sake of Jesus. Pray for their protection, pray for their families, and pray God would use their witness to bring others to faith in Christ.

Go to www.persecution.com for more information about what's happening to Christians in other countries all around the world.

Day 5
Hebrews 10:32-39

Let's be honest: When things get dangerous, or even uncomfortable, we can get scared. That's okay. Anyone in an intimidating situation will feel that way. The author of Hebrews knew that, so he encourages his readers to stand firm. Jesus isn't asking you never to fear; he's asking you to stand firm even when you're afraid. This is called *perseverance*. It means not giving in when you really want to. All of us will face moments we think we can't handle. If you stand firm, convinced that Christ is with you, then you'll be surprised what you can endure. This is the essence of faith: Refusing to give in because you know God is watching over you.

Look in this passage and find the reasons why you can stand firm.

Ask God to show you how to have faith in hard situations.

WEEK 8
ONE COMMUNITY: SHARING AMONG BELIEVERS

MEMORY VERSE

"Be devoted to one another in brotherly love. Honor one another above yourselves." (Romans 12:10)

INTRODUCTION

Growing up in my church, the word *fellowship* meant some sort of post-worship-service gathering that involved food and coffee. And that was about it. It seemed pointless then; but looking back, I can see how important those times were. A church is a family made up of different types of people. And the only way such a diverse group can become a real family—and not just a crowd—is by spending time together.

This week we'll see the members of the early Church giving money to one another, sharing their possessions, and taking care of each other. This is what a real church family is supposed to look like. But how do we get there?

In every church God wants to build something called *community*, the sense that we're all connected in a real way. Serving each other, helping, loving, and giving are all ways we express real community.

Believe it or not, this can be the most exciting and life-changing aspect of your church experience. But community isn't easy to come by. It takes a deliberate choice to be a part of the people of God. Once you join, the benefits are endless. This week we're going to look at how to build real community in our own churches.

DAILY DEVOTIONS

Day 1
Acts 4:32-37

Sharing isn't natural. No one has to teach a child to be selfish with his toys. That trait just comes naturally to him. But it applies to teenagers and adults as well. So how do you figure 3,000 people voluntarily selling their possessions to help other people? When the Spirit of God moves, we discover how the Spirit provides all we need—including a family of parents, brothers, and sisters to help us through life. Recognizing God's provision, Barnabas gladly chose to sell his land to aid the church. Would you be willing to do the same with your stuff? Our culture is selfish; it's time we challenged the status quo by loving each other sacrificially.

Do you believe God will provide all you need—even when you help others?

Do you truly love the people in your church?

What are some ways you can serve the people in your church this week?

Day 2
Ephesians 4:25-32

If you have a brother or sister, then you know that living with other people can be tough. It can be even harder for large families to get along. So imagine the problems that can arise in a church of hundreds or thousands of people. Paul encouraged the church at Ephesus to be unified; but as happens in any family, problems sometimes arose.

Go back and read this passage carefully. Think about each command. Then ask God to help you identify any situation in which you may need to change your actions.

Remember, these aren't just rules; God is trying to help us have healthy relationships with him and one another.

Day 3
James 5:13-16

Almost everyone has secrets—sins, issues, problems we don't want to talk about. But when we pretend we don't have any struggles, we're not being truthful with our friends. One of the ways we build community is by being honest with one another. In today's Scripture passage, James commands us to confess our sins not only to God, but also to one another. Why? Because God uses each of us to help our friends in Christ. This doesn't mean we should tell everyone, but we should be accountable to a few of our trusted Christian friends. The result is a depth of friendship you may have never experienced. I know it may sound terrifying, but we have to trust that God knows what he's doing. Believe me, I've tried it and it actually works. Confessing our sins to each other is amazingly powerful.

What are some things you struggle with that you've never told anyone about?

Who are some trustworthy and mature Christians you could talk to about these things?

Pray that God would show you who these people are and give you the courage to be honest with them.

Day 4
1 Thessalonians 1:1

What can you possibly get out of an introduction? A lot, actually. Flip through your New Testament and look at the first verses of some of the letters Paul wrote. Notice anything? Paul rarely wrote a letter alone. It's always Paul and Timothy, Paul and the brothers, or Paul and Sosthenes. Why did Paul always mention these other people if he was doing all the writing? Well, Paul wasn't a loner. He knew he needed other people—his community—to fully follow God. And so do we. Walking with God isn't an isolated action.

If you had to write a letter to a group of Christians who lived far away, then whose names would you include at the top of your letter? Who's walking beside you in your Christian journey? If no one comes to mind, then maybe it's time to start cultivating more Christian friendships. Thank God for the strong Christian friends you have.

Ask God to show you ways you can grow closer to other Christians.

Day 5
Hebrews 10:24-25

I don't believe any truly rational people like to get up early. I don't. Not ever! But sometimes it's necessary. And there are a few occasions when I don't mind, such as Christmas morning. For some reason getting up early on Christmas has never bothered me. It may seem like a chore to get up and make it to church on Sundays. What's the big deal? Why do we have to do that anyway? The big deal is that it's a chance for your community to meet together, and that doesn't happen very often. The people in your church need to see you so they can encourage you, and they need you to do the same for them. The author of Hebrews knew that, and he reminds us how important it is. If we never met together, then we'd never grow into the kind of family God wants us to be. So get up! It's time to see the Church. It's time to *be* the Church!

Think about all the ways you're encouraged when you go to church.

Think about the people you can encourage. Ask God to help you remember these things each Sunday.

WEEK 9
INTEGRITY: THE KEY TO OUR WITNESS

MEMORY VERSE

"But just as he who called you is holy, so be holy in all you do." (1 Peter 1:15)

INTRODUCTION

Mahatma Gandhi was an influential Hindu leader in the early twentieth century whose life and teachings are still followed by many today. He often referred to Jesus with terms of praise, prompting someone to ask Gandhi if he wanted to become a Christian. In reply, he said, "I like your Christ; I do not like your Christians. Your Christians are so unlike your Christ." His sentiment is shared by many. How many people have been driven away from church because some Christians talk like believers but never live out the faith they preach?

The reality is that if we don't live what we say, then we lose our credibility in telling others about Jesus. When Christians lack integrity, everyone loses. What's *integrity*? Having integrity means being honest. It means saying what you mean and meaning what you say. And it's more important than you know. In the early stages of the Church, God went so far as to kill one couple who purposefully lied to their church. What happened to them was pretty drastic. But their lack of integrity threatened the Church.

As Christians we have to be diligent about making sure our lives reflect our beliefs. And since we're a part of a larger body, we have to help each other live out our beliefs as well. Even if *we* live correctly, when other believers are hypocrites, it hurts our witness. So this week we're going to talk about the integrity of not just our lives, but of the Church as well. Whether you like it or not, we're all in this together.

DAILY DEVOTIONS

Day 1
Acts 5:1-11

Most of us have done things very similar to what Ananais and Sapphira did: Commit some seemingly unimportant sin and then lie about it. So after reading this story, you should be concerned. God has every right to treat us the same way, so thank God for being merciful to us. At times we may believe we're getting away with some sin, but this story should remind us that we're not. God may choose not to use his ultimate punishment, but God won't leave our sin unchecked. Hopefully this example will remind us that our sins are more damaging than we think and prompt us to avoid those sins.

Are there any sins in your life that you consciously overlook or accept? Why?

Ask God to show you where you're failing, and thank God for his grace and forgiveness.

Day 2
Job 27:6

I will maintain my righteousness and never let go of it; my conscience will not reproach me as long as I live.

Job was a righteous and determined man. Even in the face of all kinds of serious trouble, heartache, and terrible loss—including the deaths of members of his family—Job resolved to keep his faith in God. He also made up his mind to maintain an upright approach to life when most of us would have given up on God. Okay, maybe none of us will ever face the kind of hurt and pain that Job endured, but in the same way none of us is immune to life's curveballs and just plain bad stuff. (Anyone who says becoming a Christian means you're immune from hurt is lying!) So it's not a question of avoiding pain—it's a question of how we respond when pain (or anger or disappointment) enters our lives.

Do you have the kind of integrity that endures—even when times are tough and your faith is tested?

Are you ever tempted to ditch your faith or lash out at others after you've been dumped on—and even though you've been living the best Christian life you could?

If you're struggling in this area, ask God to give you the strength to endure the pain and continue to learn from Jesus' example.

Day 3
Revelation 3:14-18

I used to believe this passage meant I should be hot and never cold for God. But read it again. The problem in Laodicea isn't that they were wicked people; it's that they weren't really...anything. They talked a good game, but they were wishy-washy when it came to following God. God basically said to the church at Laodicea, "If you believe something, then act on it!" God says the same to us. If we claim to be Christians, then we can't afford to be halfhearted, saying one thing but never living it. It's not enough to simply avoid big sins and live with the little ones. It dishonors God and sends a message to everyone we know that God isn't that important to us.

How's your temperature? Would you say you're hot, cold, or lukewarm? Why?

Ask God to help you get off the fence and move toward a more focused walk with him today.

Day 4
Ephesians 5:1-8

Paul used an interesting phrase in this passage. He says there shouldn't be even a hint of sexual immorality among God's people. Many Christians ask, "Well, how far can I go? How far is too far?" We're asking the wrong questions; we're trying to get as close as we can to sin instead of safeguarding our integrity. God isn't opposed to sex; God honors sexual expression within the bounds of marriage. Until we marry, we're not to risk losing our integrity by pushing the envelope physically. If we ignore Paul's advice, then we'll find ourselves regretting the sins we knew we should have avoided and paying the consequences.

What decisions have you made to remain sexually pure?

Who helps you stay true to those commitments?

Day 5
Titus 2:3-8

Is what you do really important? Paul gave some good advice to Titus, a young pastor: Keep pure. But for ordinary people like us, it's not as important, right? Actually it is. Twice in this passage, Paul tells us to live holy lives, and then he gives us a reason: When people try to say bad things about us, they'll have no grounds for it. In fact they'll look like the evil ones because there's nothing bad to say about us. Our integrity is important because it paves the way for the gospel. If we're hypocrites, then no one will listen to us when we try to tell them about Jesus. When our lives reflect what we believe, it opens the door for people to hear what we say about Christ.

Do you know people who won't believe in Christ because of the behavior of Christians they know?

What can you do to change that image? Ask God to give you an opportunity to do that this week.

WEEK 10
AN INVINCIBLE CHURCH:
PERSECUTION OF THE APOSTLES

MEMORY VERSE

"Peter and the other apostles replied: 'We must obey God rather than men!'"
(Acts 5:29)

INTRODUCTION

Let's think for a moment about all the religions that have come and gone. There were Egyptian gods, that whole druid thing, and how can we forget all those Greek gods?

But then there's the Church. Not only has the Church stood the test of time—spanning more than 2,000 years of history—but multitudes of people have also tried to destroy it without success. Bibles have been burned, apostles executed, an entire empire tried to wipe out the Church—all to no avail. The Church continues to thrive. Why? Because Jesus is the Lord of lords and the King of kings. Impostors fade away while Christ remains.

The situation has been the same from the Church's beginning. In Acts the apostles were threatened by religious and government authorities, thrown in jail, and beaten. But none of this put a dent in God's unfolding plan for his kingdom in the world. The Church continued to grow through all of the opposition.

Today's Church is the same way. Christians around the world are persecuted, and the Church of Jesus Christ still stands. Yet most of us don't see the Church as the invincible body it is.

DAILY DEVOTIONS

Day 1
Acts 5:17-32

The apostles were jailed, freed by an angel, captured again, and brought before the people who imprisoned them. But through all of this, they didn't even begin to water down their message. In fact, they did just the opposite. When asked why they'd violated orders, they basically said the only One they obeyed was God. What if we had the same attitude? What if we weren't afraid of offending people or didn't care about our reputations? What if we were bold like the apostles and shared our faith without worrying about the consequences? Does this sound extreme? Truth is, this is exactly what the Church is supposed to be doing. God has given us the power. What are we doing with it?

As a Christian in today's society, you'll face persecution. What can you learn from today's story about the apostles?

God made you spiritually invincible. Pray that God will give you a spirit of boldness.

Day 2
Acts 9:31; 12:24; 13:52; 16:5

You may not know the whole story of Acts, but flip through the headings and see what's going on. You'll see stonings, persecutions, and danger.

Yet look at today's verses. These are like chapter markers in the book of Acts showing how the gospel continued to spread. No matter what happened, the Church continued to grow and thrive. Why? Because God was with them. God never said following Jesus would be easy, but God did say he'd be with us. As the hardships increased for the early Church, the power of God sustained them and even helped them to grow stronger. The same can be true for us today. When we seek to serve God together and refuse to let circumstances stop us, we can count on the power of God to make our lives and churches just as powerful.

What obstacles have hindered your church or youth group?

Are these insurmountable problems?

Ask God to empower your church as the churches in Acts were empowered.

Day 3
Romans 1:16-17

Why is the Church so powerful? It's not because of the people. Some individuals can command a crowd or get things done politically. But the power of the Church doesn't come from strong personalities; it comes from the gospel itself. You may feel weak or inadequate when trying to share the gospel, but you don't have to. The gospel is powerful all by itself. When you're witnessing to others, concentrate more on the gospel and less on your shortcomings. They're not as limiting as you might think. When our lives and our churches are committed to Christ, we don't need to be ashamed of anything.

Have you ever been ashamed of the gospel? Why?

How does this passage give you confidence to share your faith?

Day 4
Matthew 16:13-18

In today's passage we discover that hell (*Hades* is another word for hell) cannot stand up to the power of the gospel. But notice it's not just the gospel, but also the Church that will never be defeated. Once we join Christ, we join his body—the Church. And as a part of Christ himself, we don't have to fear the power of death or hell. They can't overpower us. The Church—your church—is much more powerful than you realize. We sell ourselves short when we assume we can't do anything in the world. But when we realize just how strong we are, hell will tremble as we accomplish God's will.

How does this passage change the way you look at your own church?

Are there any places in your life where you just assumed you were defeated?

Ask God to show you how strong you are as a part of his Church.

Day 5
2 Corinthians 11:22-33

Can this be right? I don't know about you; but after the first two shipwrecks, I'd hesitate before getting on any more boats. But Paul was unstoppable. It didn't matter what he went through; he refused to back down. What makes a man do that? What makes someone willingly walk into a dangerous situation? In verses 28 and 29, Paul showed us why. He was so passionate about the Church that it was more important to him than his own comfort. God changed Paul's life and saved him from hell, and Paul wanted everyone to know that joy. God may never ask you to do things like this, but what would you be willing to endure just to tell someone about the gospel? The Church is invincible, but it can be weakened in the short term if we refuse to attempt the tasks God has set out for us.

What are some of the sacrifices you have to make in order to share the gospel?

Ask God to give you a passion that can't be quenched by bad circumstances.

WEEK 11
SHARED MINISTRY: CHOOSING THE SEVEN

MEMORY VERSE

"Let us not become weary in doing good, for at the proper time we will reap a harvest if we do not give up." (Galatians 6:9)

INTRODUCTION

Moses was tired. He'd been listening to one disagreement after another. I imagine him mediating a dispute between two people who claim to have created manna soup, and both want the patent on the recipe. The Israelites had been coming to Moses with these kinds of questions all day, and the line still wrapped around the tent—twice. *This is ridiculous*, he thought. *I can't keep this up.* But he was the leader of Israel—wasn't settling disputes his job? If so, then how does the leader of a million people wandering in the desert go on a vacation?

Next in line was Moses' father-in-law who had some advice of his own. "Moses, share the load. It's not all up to you." So Moses did, and he got that vacation.

Just like Moses, the apostles figured out early on that they couldn't do ministry by themselves. So God helped them choose others to share the ministry of his kingdom. Everyone in the early Church had a part to play in ministry.

This week we're going to think about the shared ministry of the Church. Whether you know it or not, God has a place for you to serve, and the whole concept of church won't work unless you get involved. It's time we all got off the pews and into the game.

DAILY DEVOTIONS

Day 1
Acts 6:1-7

Michael Jordan is arguably the greatest basketball player of all time. But not even Jordan could have won a single game without his teammates. It's a lesson the Church should take to heart. God called the apostles to a specific task, but many other tasks needed to be done. Unless other people stepped up to the plate, the work wouldn't get done. God isn't about superstars hogging the entire ministry. In fact, when we let only a few people do the work, much less gets done. So if we're truly supposed to accomplish God's will, then we each have to find our place to serve—and then work at it with all of our hearts.

Do you see yourself having a vital role in your church? If so, what is it?

How can you fulfill your specific task for the kingdom today?

Day 2
1 Corinthians 12:12-26

I have no idea what my spleen does. I've never seen it, and, to be honest, I hope I never do. But I thank God that I have one. I like my spleen. My body—and life itself—wouldn't be the same without it. If the Church is a body, then that means there's a place for hundreds of different types of gifts. And if this body is going to function correctly, then we need all the people who have those different gifts to be in place and working properly. You may not believe your particular function in the church is all that important; but without your participation, everyone will suffer. God doesn't reserve ministry just for the paid church staff; all of us have a part to play. Like the spleen, you may have a role that not many other people see. But the fact that our vital organs aren't visible doesn't make them unimportant.

Do you tend to downplay your importance in the church? Why?

How can you use your gift in a way that fits with others using their gifts?

Day 3
1 Timothy 4:11-16

Paul's letters to Timothy are different from the others he wrote. Letters like the one he wrote to the Ephesians, for example, were addressed to the whole church. But Paul's letters to Timothy were written just to him. So if it's advice for Timothy, then why are we reading it? I always wondered if I had to do the things Timothy was told to do since I'm not a pastor like he was. But Paul knew more people should read this letter, so he wrote it accordingly. And God must have wanted us to read it today since it appears in the Bible. That being said, when Paul tells Timothy not to neglect his gift, everyone in the church is reminded not to neglect their God-given gifts and ministries.

Reread the passage and ask God to show you how this applies to you today.

Are you neglecting your gift(s)? How?

What can you do to use them in the church?

Ask God to help you do that today.

Day 4
Galatians 6:2

We should try to memorize this verse. It shouldn't take too long, but practicing it may take a lot longer. When we sit in a pew on Sunday, it's easy to get the idea that it's up to the pastor and paid staff members to do all the real work of ministry. We're just here to help when we can, right? Not according to Paul. Echoing the words of Jesus, Paul reminded us that everyone should be involved in helping others. That means teaching one another, encouraging one another, serving one another, and praying for one another. You probably like one of these ministries more than the others. If so, then you should make sure you work in that ministry to help others. This is the law of Christ: To love each other as we love ourselves. The church staff will never be able to do this without our help.

How are you carrying others' burdens?

Ask God to show you how he can use you in the lives of others today, then keep your eyes open for opportunities.

Day 5
Acts 6:1-10

On Day 1 this week, we saw how the apostles selected seven men to clean tables and take care of the elderly in the church. You may have thought to yourself, *I'm glad I don't have that job.* (I had the same reaction.) But one of these men—Stephen—not only was taking care of the widows, but also he was doing miracles. Since God was with him, Stephen saw the power of the Holy Spirit in everything he did. But even so, he didn't mind cleaning tables. No job in the kingdom is beneath us. Since Jesus washed feet, we have no room to refuse whatever God asks us to do. When we all serve willingly and wherever God places us, we might start to see miracles as well. God has many plans in store for you, so don't judge a ministry opportunity too quickly.

Have you ever declined a chance to serve because it was "beneath you"? What was it? Would you respond the same way now?

Are you willing to do whatever God asks of you? Why or why not?

WEEK 12
THE MARTYRDOM OF SAINTS: THE STONING OF STEPHEN

MEMORY VERSE

"But Stephen, full of the Holy Spirit, looked up to heaven and saw the glory of God, and Jesus standing at the right hand of God. 'Look,' he said, 'I see heaven open and the Son of Man standing at the right hand of God.'" (Acts 7:55-56)

INTRODUCTION

Tertullian, a church leader in the second century, said, "The blood of the martyrs is the seed of the church." He was living through times of intense persecution, yet he saw the Church continue to grow and thrive. No matter how many Christians lost their lives, the Church continued to expand.

This kind of persecution began with the martyrdom of Stephen. When faced with a mob that wanted to destroy the fledgling Christian Church, Stephen gave bold witness to Jesus Christ. In response the enraged mob stoned him. His death wouldn't be the last, either. Throughout the history of the early Church, people gave their lives for the gospel: Stephen, James, Peter, Paul. Yet the Church continues to multiply again and again.

This kind of martyrdom does not exist just in the Bible. As you read this, people all over the world are still giving the ultimate sacrifice in order to spread the gospel of Christ. You and I may never be asked to make that sacrifice, but daily we'll be asked to give our lives to Christ as we serve him wherever he chooses to use us. This week we're going to ask the question: Would I be willing to give my life for Christ? Until we understand the sacrifice of past saints, we won't be able to follow in their footsteps today.

DAILY DEVOTIONS

Day 1
Acts 7:54-60

Stephen gets credit for being the first Christian martyr. Why did Stephen have to die? Jesus came to earth to die, but that wasn't the end of his story. He endured the cross because he knew reality beyond this world exists, and his ultimate goal is within that other reality. That's where he wants us to set our goals as well. Stephen understood this, and he never asked why. Stephen's response to his coming death was almost identical to Christ's death on the cross. When Stephen saw Jesus, it was a reminder that God was pleased with his actions, and God had everything under control. As we deal with persecution, we must remember there's more to life than what we now experience.

How does understanding our final destination change the way we deal with pain and suffering here on earth?

Ask Jesus to show you how to live with your real future in mind.

Day 2
Philippians 1:19-26

Paul made the ultimate sacrifice when Nero executed him because of his Christian faith. But here we get a glimpse of Paul's attitude about martyrdom. Paul had that long-term view we talked about yesterday, and he wanted to be with Christ. But he also knew that as long as he remained here, he could serve the God he loved with his whole heart. Paul's goal was not simply a long life; it was a productive life. Ultimately he just wanted to be wherever God wanted him to be. There's more to your life than simply living. Paul understood, as we all should, that every minute we live surrendered to Christ will benefit not only us, but also everyone we come in contact with.

How would your life be different if you thought the way Paul did?

How are you using the time you've been given to help others know Christ?

Day 3
Acts 12:1-7

This is a potentially confusing passage because it raises the question why. Why did God allow James to be killed yet send an angel to save Peter? Why does God allow anyone to die for her faith? We can't fully understand the answers to these questions now, but we can trust God's character. God doesn't "play favorites" or save the lives of those he "likes better." God has a plan that works out for the best, and that plan has glory and paradise waiting for all of us who are in God. How we get there is up to God—not to us. We may not get the answers we want in terms of why things happen the way they do, but we can always trust God in spite of our circumstances.

When you're confused, where do you go for answers?

Do you go to God with your questions? Why or why not?

Spend some time talking to God about things you don't understand and about why things happen the way they do.

Day 4
2 Timothy 1:8-12

In verse 12, Paul shows us another reason why he wasn't afraid to give his life for Jesus: Paul had given it up already. Paul was firmly convinced that his old self had died when he became a believer and that he had become a brand-new person. That being the case, no one could take Paul's life from him since he'd given it up years ago. His new life was in Christ; therefore, whatever Christ asked him to do, Paul would do. With this attitude Paul could walk through danger with confidence. In his mind he believed he was already dead and his new life, which began at his conversion, was waiting for him after death. Knowing God is trustworthy gave Paul the confidence to follow Jesus even to his own earthly death.

Have you given your whole life to Jesus? What parts have you kept back for yourself?

Are you convinced God will take care of you no matter what?

Does your life reflect that?

Day 5
2 Timothy 4:6-8

Paul knew he probably wouldn't return from Rome. He'd been saved from death many times, but now God had shown Paul that this would be the end for him. No one ever looks forward to death, but Paul found comfort in this: He'd done his best for God. What an amazing thing to be able to say—that we've fought hard and kept our faith through it all. Paul was by no means perfect; but he'd lived his life for Jesus, and he was prepared to lose his life for him as well.

Have you ever considered how you'll finish?

When God finally asks you to come home, will you be able to say the same thing Paul did?

If you were to die tomorrow, would you be pleased with your service to Christ?

Imagine what it will be like when God gives you a crown of glory for persevering in your faith.

WEEK 13
GOD'S PERFECT PLAN: THE DISPERSION OF THE CHURCH

MEMORY VERSE

"Those who had been scattered preached the word wherever they went."
(Acts 8:4)

INTRODUCTION

Have you ever seen those Magic Eye pictures? You know, the ones that look like just a bunch of jagged colors but when you stare at them in a certain way, a picture will supposedly leap out at you in 3-D? I never could see the picture; in fact, staring at it just gave me a headache. But other people would swear that right in front of me—in the midst of a bunch of chaos—was an incredible picture. I have to say it's still hard for me to believe.

Sometimes our lives will look like those pictures: Completely random, jagged edges, and totally incomprehensible. But the Bible is very clear about the fact that even when things seem totally out of control, God has his firm hand on history. God is able to work every circumstance for his purposes and his glory—at all times. In Acts 8:1-8 we see the early church face a huge wave of persecution. It looks bleak for the fledgling body of believers as they're scattered everywhere. But this period of turmoil would serve to spread the gospel faster than anything else in the book of Acts.

Even when we believe nothing can be done, God can still do whatever he wishes in order to fix the situation. As we think about God's sovereignty this week, watch how God brings a perfect plan to fruition out of what looks like complete chaos.

DAILY DEVOTIONS

Day 1
Acts 8:1-8

This could've been a bad day for the Church. One of their leaders was killed by an angry mob, and the believers were forced to flee to surrounding towns. To them it may have looked as if the church were on the brink of destruction. But in the very next verse we see what really happens: God uses this persecution to spread the message of Christ to more places. What was supposed to hurt the Church actually made it grow larger and stronger. God knew this in advance. Sometimes God allows things to happen that seem destructive. But rest assured that God knows what's going on and will redeem all things for his purposes.

What are some things in your life that you don't understand?

Ask God for the faith to trust him even when things don't seem good.

Day 2
Matthew 1:18-24

Have you ever thought about how crazy this sounds? It's positively insane. The whole goal of the Messiah's coming was to liberate God's people and save them from their sins. And we got a baby. How's that supposed to work? It's questions such as these that kept a lot of people from believing in Jesus while he was on earth. But this was God's plan from the beginning. Everyone had their own ideas about how the Messiah would save God's people, but no one saw that only through a perfect sacrifice could people be made whole. Our plans may seem grand and even God-honoring, but only God's plans will stand because only God's plans will work. God knows how to orchestrate everything for the best possible outcome, so we need to learn to trust God's plans over ours—even when we'd like to choose the path ourselves.

Do you trust that God knows how to run your life better than you do?

Who makes the decisions about how you live?

Day 3
Exodus 13:17–14:18

"Are we lost?" I'm sure many of the Israelites were complaining as they began their wanderings. To them it probably seemed as though someone was asleep at the wheel. They were taking a longer-than-necessary route, and then they turned around only to get trapped by the sea. But all of this was according to God's plan. None of them could have imagined what God was planning for the Egyptians. Because Moses was firm in his resolve to follow God, we have the record of one of the most stunning miracles in human history—the parting of the Red Sea. When God leads, he always has a reason—and a good one at that. Many times we want to grumble, as the Israelites did, that this isn't the right way to go. Instead, we should trust in God's sovereign hand to make things right even when we don't see how he'll do it.

If you'd been one of the Israelites in this story, how would you have reacted?

Ask God to help you understand his sovereignty over your life and all creation.

Day 4
Acts 9:10-19

Ananias was a believer from Damascus, and we don't read anything else about him in Scripture. But he was asked to do a difficult thing when God told him to pray for Saul. As far as Ananias was concerned, God might as well have asked him to put his head in a lion's mouth. But God was insistent, so Ananias obeyed. This was Ananias' moment to shine, and the consequences of his obedience have been shaking the whole world ever since. Never underestimate just one conversion. Human history changed when Saul was saved and adopted into the Church ("Brother Saul," Ananias called him). You may believe God's tasks for you are small, but never underestimate what God can do with one act of obedience.

Have you ever seen God use you in a way you didn't expect? How did that feel?

Spend today remembering that your actions can have eternal consequences. See what changes in your attitudes.

Day 5
Luke 18:31-34

One of God's enduring attributes is that he's a Redeemer. The word literally means "someone who buys back." In Scripture it refers to how Jesus' blood paid for our sins. Here Jesus predicted his death and resurrection, as well as the torture he'd undergo beforehand. Jesus knew this would happen—and he chose to endure it anyway. One of the most barbaric acts in history brought the most glorious miracle of all: The salvation of our souls. That's redemption. God's ways can seem difficult and even wrong to us, but God's sovereign plans are always redemptive, no matter how bad it seems at the time.

Spend some time reflecting on how God brought about so much good from something so horrible.

Ask God to help you see how he can always bring good out of circumstances, even evil circumstances.

WEEK 14
AN AMAZING CONVERSION: PHILIP AND THE ETHIOPIAN

MEMORY VERSE

"The eunuch was reading this passage of Scripture: 'He was led like a sheep to the slaughter, and as a lamb before the shearer is silent, so he did not open his mouth.'" (Acts 8:32)

INTRODUCTION

Learning to drive is an interesting experience. Typically your parent or driving instructor will take you to some deserted road or parking lot for behind-the-wheel training. Driving seems easy—press the gas to go, use the wheel to turn—but a little more finesse is involved. After a few lurching starts and screeching halts, hopefully you start to get the hang of it. Or at least your instructor prays you do before he gets whiplash.

Learning new skills takes time. The disciples had to take some time to learn to walk in the Spirit. Having the Spirit of God present with them all the time meant they'd experience amazing new opportunities and an intimacy with God they'd never experienced before.

The same can be true for us as we learn to walk in the Spirit. But as it was with the first disciples, it will take some trial and error for us to work out the kinks.

This was certainly true for Philip, one of the seven chosen to help the apostles. This week we'll learn how the Spirit worked within the encounter between Philip and the Ethiopian. Each day we'll tackle a different aspect of the story and pick ways we can learn how to respond to the Holy Spirit in our own lives. You never know—by the end of the week, you might be part of a similarly amazing story.

DAILY DEVOTIONS

Day 1
Acts 8:26-40

I don't know about you, but I'd love it if God talked to me like this. In the first three verses of this account, God spoke twice to Philip—in complete sentences and with specific instructions. Sign me up for that! But does the Spirit really speak that way today? Well, yes and no. Sometimes God has very specific things for us to do and will be very direct in letting us know. You may find yourself in a spot where you know without a doubt that God wants you to do something *right now*. The Spirit doesn't usually speak this way; but when he does, we need to be obedient and take advantage of whatever opportunity God is providing.

Have you ever experienced God speaking to you like this?

How did you know it was God?

Ask God to help you hear his voice when he's speaking to you.

Day 2
Acts 8:30-31

God didn't decide to just throw Philip at the Ethiopian to see how Philip would do. God had already been working in the Ethiopian's life and now he wanted to use Philip to seal the deal. God uses us in similar ways. When God asks you to do something, God isn't just asking on a whim; there's a reason for it. God always prepares our way. When we know this, it takes a lot of the fear out of following God. No matter how odd it may seem, God has a plan when he asks us to serve in a particular way. Always remember that you're a part of a much larger plan.

How might God be moving in the lives of the people around you?

Is God asking you to help them in any way?

Ask God to show you clearly what to do.

Day 3
Acts 8:31-35

How do you know when the Spirit is involved in something? Listen to Scripture. Here the Ethiopian is reading a passage that includes a Messianic prophecy. (It's a passage in the Old Testament that talks about Jesus.) Philip immediately knew that the Spirit was leading this man through the Word, and he explained that to him. Since the Spirit inspired the Bible, he'll often use it to keep us grounded, teach us new things, and point others to Jesus. It's possible to misuse Scripture. But if we're familiar with the Word, then we should be able to recognize the real thing when we hear it. Staying in touch with Scripture is one the best ways to accurately hear the voice of the Holy Spirit.

Has the Spirit ever taught you something through Scripture?

What was it?

Ask God to show you how to use Scripture to help others around you.

Day 4
Acts 8:34-38

The Spirit began this encounter with some hands-on involvement, telling Philip exactly where to go. Notice, however, that the story ends with Philip handling the situation. I'm sure Philip was walking in the Spirit as he explained the gospel to the Ethiopian, but Philip still did the talking. When we follow God, God's intention isn't for us to become robots to be used at a moment's notice. In other words, we aren't *possessed* by the Spirit. Instead, God points us in the right direction and enables us to accomplish the goal. God wants to involve us, not just use us. That's how we act as mature sons and daughters of God—not just infants in Christ.

If God pointed you in the right direction, would you be willing to walk with God into the task?

Look around today and see if there's anyplace God might be leading you to serve.

Day 5
Acts 8:36-39

Why was the Ethiopian so ready to be baptized? Because he knew he'd been changed. We've already seen how the Spirit came upon the apostles in the form of fire at Pentecost—marking them with the Spirit. For us it's a little different. When you got saved, you may not have seen any tongues of fire falling on your head. But the Spirit rushed in nonetheless. When you get baptized, you're having your own celebration-of-Pentecost moment. It's a symbolic act where we recognize that the Holy Spirit has changed us; we've been given new power just like the first disciples. The Ethiopian didn't get touched by fire, but he saw the water. If baptism seems boring to you, then try to look past the actual water and see the fire that's represented—the fire of the Spirit changing a person's life *forever.*

How has your life changed since you became a Christian?

How does it feel to know that what happened to the apostles is happening to you?

WEEK 15
THE APOSTLE TO THE GENTILES: THE CONVERSION OF SAUL

MEMORY VERSE

"He fell to the ground and heard a voice say to him, 'Saul, Saul, why do you persecute me?' 'Who are you, Lord?' Saul asked. 'I am Jesus, whom you are persecuting,' he replied. 'Now get up and go into the city, and you will be told what you must do.'" (Acts 9:4-6)

INTRODUCTION

You can't talk about the New Testament without talking about Paul. In fact, Christianity wouldn't be the same without the life, writings, and influence of the apostle to the Gentiles. Something happened in the life of this one man that served as a turning point in history. Acts 9:1-19 records the amazing conversion of this great man—the transformation from "Saul the zealous Pharisee" to "Paul the crusader for Christ."

Paul's influence cannot be measured. Fulfilling God's will from the beginning, Paul got to be God's vessel to take the message of salvation to all people—not just the Jews. Paul was the first missionary to the rest of us. Part average Joe, part fierce debater, and part loving pastor, Paul's unique character and background made him the perfect choice as the apostle to everyone. Furthermore, God inspired Paul in his writings. He ultimately left behind 13 letters in our Scriptures.

As you read the book of Acts, you see the depth of conviction of this persecutor-turned-true-believer. And he's everywhere: In the marketplace talking to ordinary folks, in the synagogue debating religious leaders, and on the road spreading the gospel from Asia to Europe.

This week we're going to look at the conversion of the Church's first and greatest theologian, and find out why God is still using Paul in our lives today.

DAILY DEVOTIONS

Day 1
Acts 9:1-19

This is one of the most famous stories in the Bible. In fact, it shows up three times just in the book of Acts (see chapters 22 and 26). Why so often? This was Paul's defining moment when his whole life changed. Before this point Paul thought he was working for God, but he discovered he was doing just the opposite. The great thing is that God came to him anyway. Paul knew God loved him, had forgiven him, and was sending him on a mission of great importance. He knew it would cause him pain and probably cost him his life, but it was worth it to serve a God who could love a sinner like him.

What was your conversion like?

How has it changed your life?

Who have you told your conversion story to lately?

Ask God to show you where you could share your story with someone this week.

Day 2
1 Corinthians 1:1-3, 9

I was always confused when people said they had a "calling from God." I didn't doubt them because Paul obviously had a calling. He even uses the phrase "called to be an apostle" in today's passage. But notice that we also have a general calling. In verse 2 Paul reminds us that all believers have a calling from God to be pure. And we should pursue the calling we've already received. But will God ever call you as Paul was called? Maybe. Callings are very unique, and God uses a variety of ways to help each of us understand God's specific will. Don't expect Paul's experience, though; look for God's work as it specifically relates to your own life.

Do you feel God may be calling you to some form of specific service?

Ask God to make that calling clear to you. Talk to your pastor or another respected Christian leader for guidance.

Day 3
Philippians 3:3-11

If you looked at Paul from a religious perspective, then you'd see the perfect minister. Any Israelite of that day would've envied Paul and probably assumed he was a very holy man just by his pedigree. It would be the equivalent of growing up in church, having Billy Graham for your dad, getting straight As in seminary, never getting into trouble, and always knowing the right answers in church. Paul basically had all of that going for him, but he saw it as useless. In other words, none of that stuff changed him. It was his relationship with Jesus that mattered, not his polished reputation. Anyone can think you're holy, but what matters is that you really know Jesus.

Read verses 7 through 10 again. Try to understand Paul's heart as he wrote that.

Do you feel the way Paul felt?

Ask God to help you truly know him.

Day 4
1 Corinthians 2:1-5; 2 Corinthians 10:10

We don't know what Paul looked like. From the amazing impact he had on so many people, it's tempting to imagine him as a dashing, charismatic figure. But the clues in Scripture say otherwise. Paul was most likely not very attractive, and he wasn't even the best communicator. Many speakers of that day dressed well and gave incredibly entertaining speeches. Paul was criticized for not being more like them. Paul wasn't interested in entertainment; he was interested in the power of God. Who do you listen to? If you listen only to those who entertain you, then you might hear an interesting speech, but you'll miss out on people like Paul—and that's where the real spiritual power is.

Spend some time reflecting on where God is moving around you.

Could God be moving you in unexpected ways?

Keep your eyes open for God to speak to you through anyone or anything today, not just in the places you'd expect.

Day 5
Philippians 3:12-14

It's tempting to put our leaders on pedestals. They can do more than we can, so we tend to idolize them. Because of that, we can also look down on ourselves. Paul knew the Philippians might begin thinking more of him than they should, so he reminds them that he's growing in Christ as well. Our mentors and leaders aren't better than we are; they've just had more time to work at it than we have. We'll be able to know God as well as they do if we're as diligent as they've been. They aren't superhuman; they're just committed. God uses them as role models to show us it can be done. If we follow in their footsteps, then we'll see the same power and joy in our own lives.

How are you pressing on to be like Christ?

Thank God for the spiritual leaders he's put in your life to show you the way.

WEEK 16
FROM JEWS TO GENTILES: PETER AND CORNELIUS

MEMORY VERSE

"We are witnesses of everything he did in the country of the Jews and in Jerusalem. They killed him by hanging him on a tree, but God raised him from the dead on the third day and caused him to be seen." (Acts 10:39-40)

INTRODUCTION

It's hard for me to believe people once thought the earth was flat or that it was the center of the universe. Imagine you'd believed that the earth was flat all of your life. How much would it have changed your reality if someone told you the world was actually a big ball circling a gigantic star and that all those tiny pinpricks in the night sky were stars hundreds of times bigger than the earth?

I imagine the Jews in Acts felt the same type of reality check when they found out that God wasn't interested in them only, but wanted to save the whole world. They saw themselves as "the chosen people," but now God was calling them to open the doors to allow non-Jews to receive salvation in Jesus Christ.

In Acts 10 we read that God gave Peter a specific vision to make him realize that salvation was for all people, not just the Jews. The result of this revelation was an explosion of evangelism that quickly moved beyond Israel's borders and began to echo around the world. That shockwave is still expanding as the gospel is shared with people who've never heard it.

Some people say the gospel is too exclusive since it requires belief in Jesus. On the contrary, the gospel is one of the most inclusive of all faiths because it's open to anyone who believes.

This week we'll look at the heart of God and his message of love and peace. We'll also see where we fit into God's plan as he sends his gospel to all the nations.

DAILY DEVOTIONS

Day 1
Acts 10:9-48

You have to give God credit for being dramatic. But why all the theatrics here? Because this event was a big turning point for Peter—and for Christianity. Peter had followed the Law, and as far as he understood it, there were things you could and couldn't eat. The same was true for people: Some were considered to be God's people, and some were not. In even simpler terms: Jewish people were, and everyone else wasn't. So God started with something less important (food) and then moved to something very important (people) to help Peter understand. Peter got the message: God loves all people—not just the Jews—and God wants all of them to be his people. Peter resisted this thought at first. But it was unmistakable what God was telling him, so he changed his mind. God's love is for all people, not just a chosen few.

How would you react if God asked you to change your mind about something you've always believed?

Is there any place in your life where you believe some people are more important than others? Why?

How does this passage help you deal with that?

Day 2
Genesis 12:1-3

Peter probably thought God's openness to the Gentiles was new, but God had wanted this from the beginning. Abraham was the father of the Jewish people. (Remember that children's song called "Father Abraham"?) God told Abraham that he'd father a nation and his children would be special—God's people. But look at today's passage. God told Abraham his desire: That "all peoples on earth will be blessed through you" (verse 3). This was God's plan all along—that everyone could be blessed and have a relationship with him.

If God loves everyone, then how should you treat people outside your race, color, or national background?

Pray that God will help you realize that all people are God's people and that the biggest difference is that some are lost and some are saved.

Day 3
1 John 2:1-3

Humans are diverse. We have different languages, heritages, customs, and appearances. We live in different environments. But there's one thing we all share in common: Our sin nature. It affects everyone, and in that respect it's the great equalizer. No one can say she is without sin, and no one can overcome it by her own efforts. John reminds believers to remember where they came from (they used to be lost in sin) and to keep doors open for others. Jesus came to save people who are struggling with sin. That includes everyone. If we're going to be the Church of Jesus Christ, then our doors have to remain open to everyone.

Now that you're saved, do you tend to look down on people who aren't?

Ask Jesus to show you how to love all people, not just those you love now.

Day 4
Jonah 3:3–4:4

Most of us know about Jonah's aquatic adventures (see Jonah 1 and 2), but here we find the rest of the story. When Jonah finally obeyed God and preached to the Ninevites, they changed their ways. Instead of being thrilled, Jonah pouted. He hated the Ninevites and would have rather seen them destroyed. Again, here we have an Old Testament example of God's compassion for all people, even a brutal people such as the Ninevites.

Prejudice has no place in the church because it has no place in the heart of God. If God can forgive all people, then we must as well. But if prophets can suffer from prejudice, then so can we.

If God told you to share his love with someone you really despised, could you do it?

Ask God to change your heart so you can love people the way God does.

Day 5
Acts 1:6-8

God could have sent Jesus to every part of the world to tell them about salvation, but instead God chose to send you. Part of our job as the Church is to take the message of Jesus to all those who've not heard it. There are more than 1 billion people on the planet today who literally have no idea who Jesus is. They have no hope that they can be saved from their own sin. God is sending us out—just as he sent the first disciples—to share the good news with a lost world. God loves them and desperately wants them to know salvation. If this is God's heart, then it should be ours as well.

Have you felt God calling you to share the gospel with people outside your culture?

How can you do that this week...this month...this year?

Ask God to show you where he wants to use you.

WEEK 17
A GROWING CHURCH: THE CHURCH AT ANTIOCH

MEMORY VERSE

"The Lord's hand was with them, and a great number of people believed and turned to the Lord." (Acts 11:21)

INTRODUCTION

I don't know about you, but I'm continually amazed at how quickly babies grow. You see them one month, and they're small and helpless. Then just a few months later, they're walking, talking, and generally creating havoc wherever they go.

Amazing.

Most of us have stopped growing by now, so maybe we don't appreciate this as much. I'm sure God meant for babies to stop growing at a certain point, but not the Church.

In Acts 11:19-26, we see the Church multiplying and growing exponentially as the gospel moves into new areas. This growth is explosive as the Church tears down the barriers of cultural prejudice, geographical isolation, racial division, and social opposition. This is what God desires for his kingdom—to be continually expanding and bringing more people into the knowledge of Christ.

The same Holy Spirit who inspired this expansion is continuing to work in us today. Many of the barriers faced by the early Church members still threaten us, but they can be torn down just as easily through the Holy Spirit's power.

This week we're going to find out that God wants to use us to reach the world by multiplying the number of believers in our churches.

DAILY DEVOTIONS

Day 1
Acts 11:19-26

Since we've never lived in Israel, the names of places can all run together. But the Bible records them for a reason. Antioch wasn't in Israel; it was in Syria. It was filled with Gentiles, not Jews. The gospel was bursting past the borders of ancient Israel and beginning to spread to the rest of the world. All of a sudden the makeup of the church was becoming remarkably diverse. There were people of all kinds coming into the church—so many that they were becoming a totally new entity. And once their numbers became large enough, people invented a name for them—a name you and I now share with these early followers of Christ: *Christian*.

How do you react when people who are very different from you join your church?

Do people in your school see a difference between Christians and non-Christians?

Do your actions show that Christians are different? How?

Day 2
John 4:21-26

Jews and Samaritans didn't get along. Although the Samaritans were descendants of Jews, they'd intermarried with pagan peoples and were considered not true Jews. But in today's Scripture passage, Jesus showed how the gospel overcomes such barriers. Jesus was ready to share the good news with people with whom other Jews wouldn't associate. And back in Week 13, we saw Philip go to this region to share about Jesus' resurrection (Acts 8).

If we're going to spread the gospel, then we have to tear down the boundaries that separate us from others. Factors such as race, social and economic status, and different religious beliefs sometimes keep us isolated. But as believers, we have to be willing to cross those barriers for the sake of the gospel.

What's the hardest barrier for you to overcome in sharing your faith?

Ask Jesus to help you overcome these barriers for the sake of the gospel.

Day 3
Matthew 5:13-16

No matter what our spiritual gifts are, all of us are called to share Christ with others. Some of us may be better at it than others, but each Christian has this responsibility. Are you willing to do your part? Unless we make witnessing a core value of our lives, we'll probably be distracted and never get around to witnessing to people. It's easy enough to let other people share their faith, but God wants all of us to be committed to bringing people to Christ. If the Church grows, then it will be because all of us are sharing our faith.

Spend some time thinking about why it's so important to share your faith.

Then think about some ways you can begin reaching out to the people for whom you have a burden. Write some ideas for doing so in the Journal Space.

If you don't have this burden, then ask God to give it to you.

Day 4
Acts 13:1-5

Over the course of his ministry, Paul went on three missionary journeys and covered thousands of miles sharing the gospel. He wanted the message of salvation to reach as many people as possible, and he didn't mind making a long trip to accomplish that goal. How about you? God may call you to go on a short-term mission trip or even to spend a summer away from home so you can share the gospel with others who don't know Christ. There's a lot of work to be done at home, but God's call to all of us is to take the good news to the ends of the earth. If believers don't go, then that goal won't be accomplished.

Pray about whether God wants to use you in mission work in the near future.

Pray for those who are serving as Paul did and taking the gospel to new places.

Day 5
1 Corinthians 5:9-10

The Corinthians misinterpreted Paul's advice, so he had to set them straight. Apparently they had lots of fellowship with other Christians, but no meaningful contact with non-Christians. (Sounds like churches today.) We must keep each other accountable in our churches; but sometimes churches become so self-focused that non-Christians won't go near them. God wants us among other people so they can see the difference God makes in our lives. And if we're going to be effective, then this interaction needs to be up close and personal. But don't try to do this alone. All believers need to act as one to interact with a lost and dying world. Otherwise, all our salt will end up back in the saltshaker on Sundays and have no real impact on the world on a day-to-day basis.

Do you have any contact with nonbelievers? Who?

Ask God to show you how to build positive and meaningful relationships with the non-Christians in your world.

WEEK 18
REACHING THE LOST: PAUL'S FIRST MISSIONARY JOURNEY

MEMORY VERSE

"While they were worshiping the Lord and fasting, the Holy Spirit said, 'Set apart for me Barnabas and Saul for the work to which I have called them.' So after they had fasted and prayed, they placed their hands on them and sent them off." (Acts 13:2-3)

INTRODUCTION

If you've never been outside the United States, it's tempting to assume everyone around the world lives like you do. My first mission trip to Mexico cured me of that delusion. I had the privilege of helping build small houses for people who lived in huts made out of garbage—literally. Until then, I'd never thought about the needs of those who lived so far away from my day-to-day existence. But once I saw their needs, I could never forget them. Even though their physical needs were striking, they had deeper needs than the physical ones.

This week we see God sending out missionaries to reach a lost world as Paul embarks on his first missionary journey. Some pretty amazing things happen on this trip. But the most important thing is that the message of Christ is preached to people who'd probably never heard it before. The influence of the gospel is beginning to be felt outside Judea, Galilee, and Samaria.

God never forgets about the needs of non-Christians, and God wants them all to come to faith in Christ. In order to accomplish that goal, God is sending us—all of us. No matter who we are or what our spiritual gifts are, all of us are to be involved in reaching non-Christians with the message of Jesus Christ. And until those needs are met, we all have a job to do. So pack your bags. It's time to get going.

DAILY DEVOTIONS

Day 1
Acts 13:1-12

In order to spread the gospel to people who'd never heard it, missionaries had to be sent out. In today's passage Paul and Barnabas were chosen to go, and they reached out to a Roman official. So already we see them pressing beyond the bounds of the Jewish believers. In order to reach non-Christians, we'll have to go to those outside our normal routine. That may scare you. Who knows what might happen? You're right. But what might happen is that many people could be saved—just as we see in this passage. Until we're willing to go wherever God wants, we probably won't go anywhere. We won't see any miracles, either. God is calling us all to go in some way, which means we can't stay where we are and continue doing what we're doing unless we're doing what God wants us to.

If God called you to serve in a distant land for a time, do you believe you could go?

Ask God to show you how to be open to the possibility of going out to serve.

Day 2
Acts 13:1-3

Let's think about this passage from another perspective. How would it feel to send out two of your friends to preach to others? While the church must have been excited about the prospect of more people coming to faith in Jesus, they were also losing the constant presence of these ministers in their lives. One of the ways we participate in mission work is by sacrificing our personal gain for the sake of non-Christians. God will call people from our congregations to spread the gospel in other lands. Our job is to send them and support their missionary work. It's a sacrifice not only for the missionaries, but for us as well.

Are you willing to personally sacrifice for the sake of those who don't know Jesus?

Ask God to give you a sacrificial heart today.

Day 3
Colossians 4:2-6; 2 Thessalonians 3:1-2

Not all of us are called to full-time mission work. But whether or not we actually cross the borders of another country, we can still have a powerful impact on world missions. Here Paul prayed for help, knowing the prayers of his home churches were extremely important. While he was in prison, it was a great encouragement for Paul to know he wasn't alone on the mission field but surrounded by the prayers of his friends back home. All of us at home need to pray for the safety and effectiveness of our missionaries abroad. In this way we're all involved in God's plans for the nations. Think about it—when you pray, those prayers immediately impact missionaries and non-Christians around the world.

Does your church send out or support any missionaries? Find out.

If it does, then spend some time praying for them each day this week. If it doesn't, then get a list of missionaries who have birthdays coming up and pray for them each day this week.

Day 4
Matthew 9:35-38

You don't have to go far to answer the call to reach non-Christians. Here Jesus sees a multitude of ministry opportunities in his home nation of Israel. Today there are thousands of ministry opportunities right in our own nation—even in our hometowns. Jesus described his home turf as a field ripe for harvest for anyone who's willing to do the work. Look around. Every day you interact with people who need to hear about Jesus. Try praying today for the people standing in line with you, the people you see at restaurants, and your classmates and coworkers. The greatest mission opportunity could be right in front of you.

How can you reach out to those you see on a regular basis—but don't really know?

Pray earnestly that God would use you right where you are to tell others about Jesus.

Day 5
Matthew 28:18-20; Romans 10:14-15

God's command to all of us is to go and make disciples of all nations. Someone must go to those nations because millions have never heard the name of Jesus. The Great Commission applies to all of us, so we all have a call to missions. God will call some of us to go, some of us to pray for those God sends, and some of us to give in order to meet their financial and material needs. But regardless of what our role is, we're all called to help those nations hear the good news about Jesus. The trap we must avoid is assuming that mission work is someone else's job. If no one actually goes to tell them, then they'll never be saved.

Is God asking you to go to those who've never heard God's name?

Ask one of your pastors about mission opportunities for you—both now and in the future. See what kinds of mission work are available.

Ask God how you should be involved in missions.

WEEK 19
SUPPORTING MISSIONARIES: PAUL AND BARNABAS RETURN TO ANTIOCH

MEMORY VERSE

"Paul and Barnabas appointed elders for them in each church and, with prayer and fasting, committed them to the Lord, in whom they had put their trust." (Acts 14:23)

INTRODUCTION

Before the lofty days of digital photography and fancy computer programs, we had slide projectors. On Sunday nights when I was a kid, missionaries who were home on a break (something called *furlough*) would come to church and show us a slide show about where they'd been and what God had done in their ministries. You can probably imagine how boring this was for me. I wanted amazing stories of angels, narrow escapes, and exorcisms, but the missionaries never shared those. Instead, it was just the same old stories about people being saved, lives being changed, and communities being transformed by the love of Jesus.

Of course, I'd totally missed the point. They weren't flashy, but those missionaries were literally the heroes of the faith standing before me. These people had left all the cushy comforts of home and traded them for a chance to serve Christ on the front lines and share the gospel. And while they may not have wowed me with their presentations, their spiritual impact was tremendous.

In Acts Paul and Barnabas came home from their mission trip to give the early Church their version of a slide show. Supporting the missionaries who come to your church may not be a top priority for you, but it is to Jesus.

This week we're going to see how we can support those who are called to serve on the mission field, even when we're not.

DAILY DEVOTIONS

Day 1
Acts 14:21-28

It's always good to come home after you've been away for a while. The mission field is exciting and rewarding, but it's also turbulent and tiring. Paul may have seemed like a vagabond as he went from place to place. But he knew where his home was, and he promptly returned there at the end of this first missionary journey. Imagine coming home after being gone for more than a year, and you can begin to understand how he must have felt.

Maintaining the home base is one of the ways we support our missionaries, reminding them again and again that although they may sometimes feel alone out on the field, we're always supporting them. You may not know the missionaries' names, but they need you nonetheless.

Is your church like a home to you? How can you build relationships so it becomes one?

Pray for those serving Christ away from your church home.

Day 2
Acts 14:27-28

Remember, there were no pictures back then, no videos, no Internet. These people rarely saw much outside their hometown. So for Paul to tell them what God was doing in another land was like hearing news from another planet. Letters had been their only real correspondence since Paul left, and getting a chance to hear Paul describe what God was doing in other places was a rare privilege. Sometimes we take for granted our ability to instantly see what's going on in other places. We also see and hear so much each day that we become calloused to what's truly exciting. If we aren't interested in how God is moving in people's lives around the world, then maybe we've gotten too caught up in our own little world.

What things do you consider the most exciting? Are they eternal or temporary?

Ask God to give you a hunger to know how he's impacting people around the world.

Day 3
Ephesians 4:1-13

For many people the idea of doing mission work in another country has never been appealing. And the truth is that not all of us will be called to go. The mistake we can make is to assume that if we aren't called to go, then we don't have to do anything. But in this passage, Paul reminds us that although we're given different gifts, the ultimate goal is for all of us to be unified and to grow into maturity. Unless each person uses his unique gifts, this won't happen. Translation: Unless we support those who have different callings than ours, we'll never grow to fullness in Christ. So even if mission work isn't your thing, you still need to be actively involved in supporting those who do have that calling.

How can you begin to regularly support missionaries?

Think about those with different callings from yours. Thank God for giving them their gifts and pray for their continued growth.

Day 4
1 Corinthians 9:7-15

Not all the churches were spiritually minded. Paul chided the Corinthians for not supporting missionaries. Although he wasn't asking them to support *him*, he was reminding them that they received great benefit when other churches originally sent Paul and Barnabas to them. Therefore, they should also bless others by supporting more missionaries. If supporting missionaries or taking time to pray for them ever seems to be a burden to you, then think back to all the people God has sent to help you grow: Sunday school teachers, pastors, camp counselors, youth ministers. All of these individuals were supported by someone else so they could help you. Shouldn't we do the same for others?

Have you ever had an attitude like the Corinthians'?

How can we avoid this mentality?

Spend some time thanking God for the people he's used in your life. Then thank some of them personally, if possible.

Day 5
Acts 14:27-28

Put yourself in the shoes of Joe Worshiper from Antioch. A while back the church leaders asked for an offering to help this guy named Paul. You were new to the church and didn't know him; but in obedience to Christ, you decided to give some money to help his ministry. Later, Paul returns and shares with the church that the gospel is going farther than it ever has, that churches were started in cities that had none, and that thousands had come to faith in Christ. Then he looks at you and thanks you for supporting him. Who knew that a small act of obedience could have such far-reaching results? This very scenario is played out every time we support missionaries with our money, love, and prayers.

Find out if your church has sent out any missionaries. If so, get in contact with them and find out how you can support them. If there are no missionaries serving from your church, then ask your pastor or youth pastor to help you find some you can get in touch with.

WEEK 20
HEALING A RIFT: THE JERUSALEM COUNCIL

MEMORY VERSE

"God, who knows the heart, showed that he accepted them by giving the Holy Spirit to them, just as he did to us. He made no distinction between us and them, for he purified their hearts by faith." (Acts 15:8-9)

INTRODUCTION

From a football rival to your nation's sworn enemy, it's hard to love anyone who isn't on your side—for whatever reason. The tension between two groups can grow from a minor rivalry to anger, hatred, and even violence that's sustained for centuries. This was the case for the Jews and Gentiles. The Jews were called by God to be his chosen people, and everyone else wasn't. Therefore, Gentiles, the name given to any non-Jew, were typically excluded from most Jewish ceremonies and were considered unclean.

So imagine the surprise of the Jewish Christians when Gentiles began receiving the same Holy Spirit they'd received. "You mean, God loves them, too?" Paul and Peter had begun ministries to bring Gentiles into the new Church. But with the inclusion of Gentiles came a huge problem for the Jews: "How do we get along with the same people we've always excluded?" In Acts 15 we read about a heated discussion among Paul, Barnabas, Peter, James, and other apostles and elders of the church concerning this very problem.

This week we're going to look at how the early Church responded to God's call to love all people, not just the ones they were comfortable with. The challenge for the Jewish Christians is also our challenge today as God calls us to love and include everyone—even the ones we see as being on the "other side."

DAILY DEVOTIONS

Day 1
Acts 15:5-12, 22-30

This could have been a disaster. Strong opinions were held on both sides as the Jewish Christians had to decide how to treat their new Gentile brothers and sisters. In the end the leaders decided that no matter what they thought before, they had to follow where God led. Conflict is inevitable since God is continually helping us to grow and change from what we are to what we need to be. In order to resolve this conflict, we have to be willing to change even the things we hold dear if God asks us to. These leaders were humble and open to the movement of God; therefore, a crisis was averted.

Are you willing to change if God asks?

What are some of the subjects God has changed your mind about?

Are you willing to obey even if you don't get your way? Why or why not?

Ask God to help you apply today's Scripture passages to your own life.

Day 2
Ephesians 2:11-22

In the temple there were warning signs posted on a low wall that told the Gentiles that if they crossed that line, they'd be killed—immediately.

And the Jews meant it. When God revealed his plan to extend salvation to their hated rivals, the Jewish Christians probably wondered why. But Paul explains that God wants a unified family, not isolated pockets of believers. God wants us together. The point of breaking down the dividing walls isn't just for the sake of tearing them down; it's to make all believers into the amazingly powerful kingdom that God wants us to be. We can't do that on our own. We need each other. We become who we're meant to be when we follow Christ—together.

Read the passage again and try to put yourself in the shoes of both the Jews and the Gentiles.

What will it take for you to join with believers you normally don't associate with?

Pray for God's guidance and help.

Day 3
Ephesians 3:1-11

Why is it so important that we love those outside our comfort zone? In verse 9 of today's passage, Paul writes that becoming unified despite the barriers that divide us sends a message to the rest of the world that God is at work. Even more amazing, Paul says it sends this message to all heavenly beings, not just humans. God is doing something in us that has never been done before. It's so new that even the heavenly hosts are shocked to see how God could bring such different groups of people together in Christ. It's not easy, but the impact of our unity has cosmic proportions. Have you ever considered how important your actions are in the grand scheme of things?

If you knew your actions had cosmic impact, how would it change your priorities and choices?

Name someone outside your comfort zone who you can reach out to today.

Day 4
Galatians 2:11-14

Change doesn't always stick. In yesterday's Scripture we saw how Peter made the right call by standing up for Gentile believers. Today we read how Peter slipped back into his old ways, and Paul rightfully challenged Peter to return to the right path. Peter and Paul were friends and partners in sharing the gospel. Are you willing to do the same for your friends when they backslide? People may know the right decision but still make a bad choice. In those times they may need us to help them stand firm when they're pressured to backslide. We're not the Holy Spirit, but we're called to help one another stay on track when times are tough.

Has anyone ever confronted you about something you did? How did you respond?

Is God asking you to help a friend stay on the right path?

How can you do that in a loving manner?

Day 5
Colossians 3:12-14

Sometimes it's hard to move beyond old anger. Whether someone hurt you or maybe you just never got along with a person, it's not easy to shake hands and be friends. God doesn't expect you to pretend that you and your old enemies don't share a past, but God does expect you to forgive them and move toward unity. Even if it takes time, we should be committed to allowing old wounds to heal so we can be unified as believers in Christ. Let go of the grudges, stop bringing up the past, and give someone another chance. Over time, God will heal the old wounds and replace them with unity among people who are really Christians.

Is there any past history that's building a wall between you and another believer?

What would it take for you to begin moving on from that hurt?

Ask God to help you begin to heal.

WEEK 21
VALUABLE FOR SERVICE: PAUL AND BARNABAS' DISAGREEMENT

MEMORY VERSE

"Some time later Paul said to Barnabas, 'Let us go back and visit the brothers in all the towns where we preached the word of the Lord and see how they are doing.'" (Acts 15:36)

INTRODUCTION

There are a few misconceptions about the Christian life that we ought to clear up right away:

> *Misconception #1: Pastors don't sin. They're perfect and should be expected never to fail. While most pastors are great people and should be held to a higher standard, they still sin, and they also fail. So if you expect them to be perfect, then you're going to be disappointed.*

> *Misconception #2: Real Christians always get along and never fight. Even though two Christians may sincerely try their best to walk with Christ, they can still have conflicts with each other. It's just one of those pesky consequences of not being perfect and living in an imperfect world.*

Thankfully, the Bible doesn't whitewash conflicts between believers, even when they involve our most respected leaders. Acts 15 records one of these altercations between Paul and his friend Barnabas over yet another leader—John Mark.

Whether we like it or not, we're going to have to deal with conflict—and not just with unbelievers, but also with our brothers and sisters in Christ. It's hard and uncomfortable; but if we choose to look to Christ for help and not to allow our feelings to guide us, then we can usually find a godly compromise.

This week we'll look at how Paul and Barnabas responded to each other and how they ultimately resolved their conflict. Hopefully, we'll gain some insight into how we can handle conflict in our own lives as well.

DAILY DEVOTIONS

Day 1
Acts 15:36-40

I thought that if you're really following God, then you'd never have any disagreements. Umm...no. Even when we're seeking God sincerely, we can still be wrong—or at the very least, we can fail to see the best path to take. Even though Paul and Barnabas were friends and were involved in an amazing ministry together, this disagreement drove them apart. Conflict will occur in all relationships—even with your best friends. When this happens you sometimes have to be willing to leave your own desires and selfishness at the door and ask God to guide you. Then you must follow God as best you know how, even if it means parting company for a while.

How do you deal with conflict?

Do you ask God for guidance or do you simply do whatever you believe is right?

Ask God to be the mediator of your conflicts with others.

Day 2
2 Timothy 4:9-12

Whatever grievance Paul had against John Mark in the past, in today's passage we see that Paul forgave him and moved on. People—even those we love and care about—are going to let us down in this life, but we can't just write people off when they fail us. If we do, then we'll miss out on what God is doing in their lives and the blessings God wants to bring to us through them. Paul was willing to look past old hurts and allow forgiveness to heal their friendship. He also recognized that John Mark was a fine leader and that his past history shouldn't keep them from working together.

Has someone ever let you down big-time? When?

Did you mend your friendship with that person?

If not, then are you willing to allow God to heal your relationship with that person in the same way Paul did with John Mark?

Ask God to help you forgive those who've let you down.

Day 3
John 21:15-19

Peter made lots of mistakes. He was brash. He talked when he should've kept quiet. And right before this conversation with Jesus, Peter denied Jesus three times. Not the picture of the most qualified person to lead the early church. Yet Jesus knew Peter would make it. Jesus was able to look beyond Peter's faults to see the leader Peter was becoming. We can avoid a lot of conflicts in our relationships when we're able to be patient with others' mistakes. And if you ever get tired of putting up with their failures, then remember they're doing the same for you.

Ask God for patience to deal with people—especially those you don't get along with.

Spend some time praying for them and about your attitude toward them.

Day 4
1 Peter 5:13-14

We're pretty familiar with John Mark by now, but you may be more familiar with him than you realize. While John Mark initially offended Peter and went his own way for a while, he ultimately became a very influential member of the Church. Here we find him serving with Peter, and tradition tells us that John Mark is the author of the gospel of Mark. But if John Mark wasn't a disciple, then how did he know what Jesus said and did? He heard it all from Peter. Even though John Mark made some relational mistakes early in his ministry, God still had huge plans for this young man—plans that have been helping believers for more than 2,000 years. Never underestimate what God can do with willing hearts—even those who've made mistakes in the past.

Could God use you like he did John Mark? Why or why not?

Ask God to help you learn from your mistakes so you can continue to serve wherever you're sent.

Day 5
Colossians 4:10-11

Here we see an incident that took place several years after the events we read about on Day 1. John Mark is now serving Paul while Paul is serving time in a Roman jail. John Mark had chosen to abandon Paul earlier in his life, but here he was serving with him again. Everyone makes mistakes, but even a mistake like this doesn't disqualify you from ministry. Like John Mark, we can't let our past failures hinder us from learning from our mistakes, repenting, and growing as Christians. John Mark's willingness to make amends with Paul and rejoin him in ministry shows us that even though conflicts will occur, resolution is always possible if both parties are willing to forgive and move on.

Don't let embarrassment over past failures keep you from enjoying a godly friendship.

Have you ever done something that you believed disqualified you from being used by God?

Have you repented and gotten back on track? You can! Ask God to help you do that now.

WEEK 22
REBUKING IN LOVE: PAUL'S DISAGREEMENT WITH PETER

MEMORY VERSE

"I have been crucified with Christ and I no longer live, but Christ lives in me. The life I live in the body, I live by faith in the Son of God, who loved me and gave himself for me." (Galatians 2:20)

INTRODUCTION

"Rebuke in love." Somehow those words don't seem to go together. Kind of like some other oxymorons, such as "jumbo shrimp" or "civil war." How can you rebuke someone and love her at the same time? But this is what God asks us to do when we face problems with other believers.

As Christians we're all still wrestling with our sin nature even though we've been set free from sin. That being the case, there will be times when we have to confront Christian friends—when they gossip to us about others, when they make dating decisions that are scripturally wrong, when they act out of anger instead of love or forgiveness. But do we have to confront them? And if we have to, then how do we confront them? Can't we just pray for them? Actually, no.

Paul illustrates this point well, since he personally dealt with this issue on many occasions. On a return trip to Jerusalem, Peter began backing off from his convictions about Gentiles being allowed equal access in the church. So Paul boldly confronted him about it and the matter was resolved. Paul then wrote to the Galatians about the incident—not to gloat, but because they were committing the same sin.

Two things are certain: There will be conflict, and we have to be involved in resolving it. We do have a choice, though, in how we handle these situations. This week we're going to look at how to handle conflicts among friends.

DAILY DEVOTIONS

Day 1
Galatians 2:11-21

How's this for a tense moment? What do you do when Peter and Paul—two of the most famous church leaders of all time—have a disagreement? Paul knew Peter was tempted to drift back into his old ways, but those old ways jeopardized the gospel. It would have taught people to live by works instead of grace. To Paul, the gospel was worth defending, even though it meant rebuking Peter in public. And in Peter's letters we see no hostility whenever he mentions Paul. So we know this event didn't ultimately divide them. The real question for you is this: Would you confront a friend in order to defend the gospel?

Is the gospel worth jeopardizing a friendship over? Why or why not?

Ask God to show you how to balance patience, love, and confrontation.

Day 2
1 Corinthians 5:9-12

How many times have we heard the phrase, "But who am I to judge someone else?" While this is great advice for those outside the church, Paul reminds the Corinthians that if someone claims to be a believer and then lives a lifestyle that's obviously contrary to Scripture, then we have an obligation to help bring that person back to a right perspective. It's not an option; it's a command. It's obviously difficult to do this and much easier to ignore the situation. But ignoring it only makes things worse and leaves a Christian brother or sister in the bondage of sin. If we love one another, then we must learn to help each other remain faithful—even if that means confronting each other in love when necessary.

What are some reasons we don't confront other believers in love?

Are they valid reasons?

Pray about any situations in which God might have you confront someone in love. And ask for God's wisdom regarding what to say.

Day 3
James 5:19-20

Some people just like to argue and want to be right all the time. You may know someone like that who seems to confront everyone about everything. But God doesn't tell us to confront others so we can be right and tell them they're wrong. The goal is to save them from the destructive power of sin. If this isn't our goal in rebuking someone, then we don't have the proper attitude. Before you talk to someone about his problem, ask yourself why you're doing it. Is it really to help him, or is this really about you? Remember, we have to rebuke others in love—not for our pride, not to make a point, and not because we don't like them. Check your motives before you confront someone.

Think through the last confrontation you had. Why did you do and say the things you did and said?

Ask God to fill you with the Holy Spirit so you'll be able to rebuke in love, rather than for selfish reasons.

Day 4
Matthew 18:15-17

When Jesus tells us how to confront each other (notice that he knows it will happen among believers), he covers all the bases we've talked about so far. First, he shows us that sin shouldn't go unchecked; it needs to be confronted in the church. Second, he talks about our brothers. This isn't an academic exercise; it's a chance to love our brother (or sister) and bring him (or her) back into a right relationship with God and the church. Third, he suggests that we include others in the process. By doing so we make sure that we're not confronting someone out of spite. Having others there who are objective about the situation keeps our emotions in check. Is this process easy? No! But this is the kind of game plan that works.

Have you ever tried this method when dealing with a conflict? How did it go?

Ask God to show you how to walk through each step of the process correctly and prayerfully when you're confronting someone.

Day 5
Galatians 6:1-5

Confronting our friends is no easy matter. It's messy and it can be hurtful. But Paul reminds us that it can also be dangerous. God calls us to help our brothers and sisters get out of their sinful patterns, and God will help us as we help them. But sometimes this means we'll be exposed to the same kinds of temptations that our friends have already fallen into. We have to keep our guard up as we reach out to struggling believers. Remember, it's always easier to pull someone down than to pull someone up. So be careful. We need to protect ourselves as we help others.

What precautions would be helpful when reaching out to struggling friends?

Pray for God's protection and help before you talk to your friends about their sins.

Pray for anyone you know who's struggling in sin today.

WEEK 23
SPIRITUAL PARENTHOOD: PAUL'S SECOND MISSIONARY JOURNEY AND TIMOTHY

MEMORY VERSE

"So the churches were strengthened in the faith and grew daily in numbers."
(Acts 16:5)

INTRODUCTION

Babies require a lot of attention...in the morning, in the afternoon, and at night. If you don't believe me, ask a new parent.

Spiritual babies are the same way: They also require a lot of attention. When people come to faith in Christ, they don't wake up the next morning with all the answers. In fact, new believers' questions keep multiplying. So it's a good thing there are mature Christians around to help them.

In addition to our biological parents, God provides spiritual parents to show us how to grow in Christ. Your spiritual parent may be your pastor, youth minister, or a good Christian friend. Spiritual parents are crucial to your spiritual growth.

Paul played this role for a young man named Timothy. In Acts 16 Paul, already on his second missionary journey, decided to bring Timothy along. And then Paul basically spent the rest of his life mentoring Timothy. Paul became Timothy's spiritual parent and helped him mature in the faith.

As you grow spiritually, God desires for you to parent other young believers. In fact, you should always have at least two types of people in your life: Someone who's discipling you (a "Paul"), and someone you're discipling (a "Timothy"). This week we're going to see how the early Christians parented each other so we can begin to do the same.

DAILY DEVOTIONS

Day 1
Acts 16:1-5

Thus begins one of the greatest partnerships in history. Timothy became Paul's right-hand man and carried the torch after Paul was martyred. Paul wasn't interested in just telling people about Jesus; he was also interested in preparing someone to take his place. Timothy's dad most likely wasn't a believer, so Paul took Timothy in and trained him like a son. Because of this long-term personal treatment, Timothy became a trusted friend and minister in his own right. God is calling us not only to spread the gospel, but also to train those who are less spiritually mature to walk with Christ. No matter where you are in your journey, you can always help those who are younger in the faith.

Who are some of your spiritual mentors?

Who are some of the younger believers you help—or could help—in their walk with Christ?

Day 2
Mark 5:37; 9:2; 14:33-34

While Jesus spent his years of ministry preaching and teaching all over Israel, he also poured a lot of time into his 12 disciples. And from among those 12, there were three with whom he spent extra time. Jesus knew it would take more than mass preaching to bring about the kingdom of God. It would require lifelong relationships. Ultimately, Jesus' grand plan for discipleship was not telling the entire world about his Father, but investing his life in a few souls who'd turn around and invest their lives in others who'd do likewise until the task was accomplished.

Is someone pouring her life into you—like Jesus did with the disciples?

If not, then pray that God would send such a person into your life.

Ask God to show you someone into whom you can begin pouring your life as well.

Day 3
Titus 2:3-5

Whose job is it to be a spiritual parent? It's easy to believe that teaching others how to be godly is a pastor's job—or at least someone with more experience. Almost everyone thinks that way. But if you wait until you believe you're ready to teach others, then you'll never actually teach anyone. Paul exhorts Titus to encourage the women in the church to train the younger women. It's not just a job for a few, but it's a job for every person in the church. The same could be said for the men of the church. Mentoring younger believers is everyone's job, including yours. Don't worry; Jesus isn't asking you to be a spiritual parent to everyone, but keep your eyes open for the few people you could impact in a special way.

How can you begin mentoring younger believers in your church?

Is there anything in your life that would hinder you from taking on such a role? What is it?

Ask God to help you deal with it immediately.

Day 4
Philippians 1:3-11

Paul was no fly-by-night con artist. When he'd plant a church, he'd often spend months or even years helping the people get the church on its feet before he moved on. Because of his personal investment, those churches were very dear to Paul's heart. Their members were like sons and daughters to him. Many of the letters we read in the New Testament are letters Paul wrote to the churches he'd started. Even though he couldn't be with them physically, he wanted them to know he loved them, prayed for them, and was thinking about them. Your encouragement can go a long way in the lives of those you love.

Who do you encourage on a regular basis?

Ask God to remind you of some people you could encourage today with a word, a phone call, or an e-mail. Then do it!

Day 5
2 Corinthians 6:3-13

Being a parent isn't easy. (Go ask your mom or dad if you don't believe me!) Sometimes even the people we try to help the most won't appreciate what we're doing for them. After all that Paul had done for them, the Corinthians still casually disregarded him. This hurt Paul just like it would hurt us if our efforts were ignored. But Paul didn't give up on them. (The letter of 2 Corinthians is proof enough of that.) When those you're trying to train don't respond as you'd like them to, remember that helping people grow is a long-term process. It's not about a one-month or two-month commitment but a lifetime of sharing your life with them. Look past your own hurt and see the big picture. The people we're trying to help will probably come around eventually, but we have to stay committed.

Have you ever been ignored after you invested a lot into someone?

How did you handle it?

Ask God to help you persevere in helping others—even when they don't give much back in return.

WEEK 24
PRAYER: FIRST LETTER TO TIMOTHY
(PART 1 OF 2)

MEMORY VERSE

"I urge, then, first of all, that requests, prayers, intercession and thanksgiving be made for everyone—for kings and all those in authority, that we may live peaceful and quiet lives in all godliness and holiness." (1 Timothy 2:1-2)

INTRODUCTION

Have you ever read about elections that were decided by only a handful of votes? It happens all the time—even in elections for the President of the United States. And with such small margins of victory, few would deny that every vote is important. Therefore, no one can honestly say it doesn't matter if he votes or not. Voting is a right and a privilege of American citizens. No matter who you are, once you turn 18, you get that right and the power that comes with it.

As believers in Jesus Christ, we have something even more powerful (and you don't have to wait until you're 18 to use it). God tells us that our prayers are incredibly powerful—a stronger force than you've ever dreamed of having. Combined with the prayers of other Christians, our prayers are an amazing force in the world.

Paul knew the importance of prayer. Paul wrote his first letter to Timothy while Paul was imprisoned in Rome, anticipating the end of his life. Looking back on his ministry, Paul knew unmistakably that the prayers of the churches were the foundation of his spiritual successes. He wanted Timothy and all of his churches to never forget how tremendously powerful the prayers of the saints are.

This week we're going to look at both the prayers of the Church and our personal prayer lives. Maybe you've never really thought about your prayer life; maybe it's just something you do. But with a force this powerful, we should expect the supernatural.

DAILY DEVOTIONS

Day 1
1 Timothy 2:1-8

It seems everyone has a political opinion today, but politicians come and go. What doesn't change is God's plan for the world and your role in that plan. Believe it or not, you're very important in bringing God's plans to fruition. When you pray for government leaders, for the advancement of the gospel in other parts of the world, or for Satan's plans to be defeated, you're making a real impact. God could do this alone, but God isn't going to. God wants to use you as well—that's God's plan. So your prayers are incredibly important—they can have worldwide impact! That means we need to be diligent in our prayers for what's going on outside our small circle of friends.

What are some global concerns of the Church that you can pray about today?

Ask God to give you a bigger picture of how your prayers affect the world around you.

Day 2
James 5:13-18

Do you ever feel as though your prayers bounce off the ceiling—that God might listen to your pastor, or to someone really holy, but not to someone like you? I believe most of us feel that way. In today's passage James encouraged the people in his church to pray—all of them. In the Old Testament, the Jews had their own version of a spiritual giant, a guy named Elijah. God answered his prayers (you can read about it in 1 Kings 17 and 18). Yet James wrote that Elijah was just a man like you and me. God wants to answer your prayers in the same way. The question is do we want to be righteous like Elijah? If we do, then there's no reason why we can't see that kind of power in our prayer lives.

When was the last time you saw God answer a prayer in your life?

Pray in faith today about something that only God could accomplish.

Day 3
Ephesians 6:18-20

By now, you've probably picked up on the fact that the Christian life isn't just about you; it's about us. If that's true, then our prayer lives should reflect that fact. In this passage Paul instructs us to have each other's backs as we fight spiritual battles each day. We must pray for one another if we want to succeed. Case in point: Paul asked the Ephesians to pray that he'd preach with boldness. Can you believe that? Did Paul really need any help? Apparently he did, and he relied on his church family for that help. In the same way, we need to be praying for our church family every day, asking God to protect us, help us grow, and use us for his glory.

Do your prayers typically revolve around you only?

How can you change that?

Who are you praying for daily?

Day 4
Ephesians 6:18

I know you read this verse yesterday, but let's think about it again. Paul tells us to pray with all kinds of prayers. Have you ever thought about the fact that there are many ways to pray? I tend to get stuck in a prayer rut: "God, could you help me with...?" Richard J. Foster wrote a book called *Prayer: Finding the Heart's True Home* (Harper Collins, 1992) that outlines 21 different kinds of prayer, such as intercessory prayer, healing prayer, prayers of suffering, and many, many more.

Today, do something different during your prayer time. Spend the whole time thanking God for all the things you have that you can see. Go outside and praise God for his creation. Sit in silence and just listen, not asking God for anything. Pray for others' needs only. Let's put this verse into practice by experimenting with prayer today. It's legal, I promise. Try it out!

Day 5
1 Thessalonians 5:17

How's that for a quick memory verse? In typical Paul fashion, he gives some final instructions to the Thessalonians and includes this command. But doesn't this sound unrealistic? How can you pray *all the time*? Wouldn't you run into things with your eyes closed? Actually, Paul meant that we should be in an active relationship with God so we can communicate with him whenever and wherever we are. A while back I started saying flash prayers when I was in public. Instead of having a formal prayer time, I kept my eyes open and prayed two-second prayers for the people I saw. I prayed, *God, show me how to encourage that person*, or *God, I pray you'll help her; she looks upset*. You can do this hundreds of times a day, and it helps you focus throughout the day. It really is possible. Give it a try!

Do you talk to God only during your prayer time? Why or why not?

Ask God to show you moments in which you can pray for others throughout your day.

WEEK 25
QUALIFIED LEADERS: FIRST LETTER TO TIMOTHY (PART 2 OF 2)

MEMORY VERSE

"Beyond all question, the mystery of godliness is great: He appeared in a body, was vindicated by the Spirit, was seen by angels, was preached among the nations, was believed on in the world, was taken up in glory." (1 Timothy 3:16)

INTRODUCTION

Most televangelists bug me. Have you ever actually listened to these guys? Some are great people of God, to be sure, but others are charlatans with a lot of charisma and very little depth. And many are masters at bending Scripture to suit their needs. It seems few of these preachers are interested in truly teaching people the Word of God; most of them seem more interested in receiving people's money.

Unfortunately, from time to time leaders who mirror the lack of character displayed by some televangelists will creep into the Church. And it's a problem that was around long before television was invented. Paul understood the danger. In his last letters, he left clear commands about how to evaluate people who want to be church leaders.

False leaders have always been a threat to the Church. But God is faithful to send us qualified leaders who can truly teach the Bible and instruct us how to be better followers of Christ.

This week we're going to look at the qualifications for being a leader in the church. We need to know this information so we can weed out the false teachers from those who can really help us. We also need to know this because God may call us to be leaders one day.

DAILY DEVOTIONS

Day 1
1 Timothy 3:1-15

Some people seem to be natural-born leaders. But being a leader means more than just being in charge. In order to be a good leader, especially a spiritual leader, you must have certain qualifications. In today's passage Paul describes some of them. Almost all have to do with character. God is more interested in you being a man or woman of God than a great speaker or a popular person. Why? Because talent can be misused. If you're a godly person, then you'll lead well because you have the character to use your gifts positively.

Have you ever wanted to lead? Why or why not?

Take a personal inventory of your character based on today's verses. Which of these traits do you need to work on?

Ask God to continue shaping your character today.

Day 2
1 Timothy 1:3-7

For most of us, leading others isn't on our to-do lists. To be honest, it can be scary to take on the responsibility of leading others. But God always needs good leaders, and he may call you to be one. God will sometimes choose people who never thought about leading to be the best leaders of all. Saul never asked to be a leader. At his coronation as the first king of Israel, Saul was so scared he hid in some luggage. (Read the story in 1 Samuel 10:17-27.) Sounds like some leader, huh? If God calls you to lead, then you need to accept the challenge and not give in to your fear. You may not feel up to the job; but if God calls you, then God will equip you. Trust God and don't fear!

Do you feel like a leader today? Why or why not?

Pray that God would reveal what may be your role as a leader in the kingdom.

Day 3
1 Timothy 3:6-7

Some people seem to have "leadership material" written all over them, but they still may not be ready to lead others. Paul reminds us that new converts aren't prepared to fill leadership positions just yet. This seems odd, since new converts are usually some of the most excited Christians we know. Why shouldn't we let them use that energy? While new Christians may be sincere and excited, they don't have the maturity to handle everything just yet. Similarly, you may have a lot of passion, but it'll take some time before God uses you as a leader on a larger scale. Also, Paul tells us that real leaders are people who are respected by outsiders as well as by those within the church. Good leaders love people no matter where they are or what they're doing.

How is your reputation among non-Christians?

Do they know that you love them and can interact with them even if you don't live like they do?

Ask God to mold your character so you can lead others.

Day 4
Psalm 51

Leaders aren't perfect. In fact if they *look* perfect, then something is probably wrong. The Old Testament is filled with examples of godly people who made sinful decisions. Moses killed a man. David committed adultery and murder. Abraham lied about his wife. But, as we see in these cases, making mistakes doesn't disqualify us from service. David wrote today's passage after he made a huge mistake and was confronted about it. The true test of a leader is one's ability to own up to sin, accept the consequences, and make changes to prevent it from happening again. Leaders are held to a higher standard, but we should always leave room for mistakes and repentance. After all, isn't that how we want our leaders to treat us?

Have you ever had a leader disappoint you? How did he respond? How did you respond?

Ask God to show you how to forgive your leaders when they make mistakes.

Day 5
Galatians 6:6

As a kid I often forgot about the giver once I got the gift. As soon as that wrapping paper was off, I was totally focused on the new toy; but I wasn't being very grateful. God has been good to provide us with lots of teachers and leaders to show us how to follow him. God also wants those leaders to be encouraged as they teach us. One of the ways we can encourage our leaders is to make sure we let them know how much we appreciate their leadership in our lives. Telling them how we're growing, reminding them that they're really helping us, and respecting their leadership are all ways we can give something back to those who give leadership to us. Let's not forget the ones who give so much to us.

How can you encourage your pastor and other church leaders today?

Spend some time praying for them and asking God to bless their ministries.

WEEK 26
THE BIBLE: SECOND LETTER TO TIMOTHY (PART 1 OF 2)

MEMORY VERSE

"All Scripture is God-breathed and is useful for teaching, rebuking, correcting and training in righteousness, so that the man of God may be thoroughly equipped for every good work." (2 Timothy 3:16-17)

INTRODUCTION

Authority is one of those words we don't particularly like. Who wants to obey people in authority? But think about what life in our country would be like without it. With no laws, people would do whatever they wanted. Imagine driving without traffic lights or stop signs. It would be chaos.

We also need a foundation—something solid to stand on, something that won't break in the midst of our problems. Our culture asks Christians, "What makes you right and everyone else wrong?" It's an honest question. The answer is we don't base our lives on our opinions or our desires. We base our lives on the Word of God. As Paul trained leaders for his churches, he spelled out why Scripture is so important for Christians. The Bible is God's unchanging foundation that shows us what truth is. It's the authority of our lives.

When God tells us through Scripture that something is right, it's right. We know this because God inspired his Word and made sure it was passed down to us accurately and unchanging for thousands of years. The foundation of the Church is also the foundation of our lives. This week we're going to look at the place Scripture has in our daily lives.

DAILY DEVOTIONS

Day 1
2 Timothy 3:14-17; 2 Peter 1:20-21

It's time for another reality check. You may have been reading the Bible for most of your life, or maybe you just picked it up. Either way, here's the question: Do you really believe it's God's Word and not just rules, not just someone's opinion, and not just an old book full of stories? If you really believe it's God's Word, then do you obey it? If we believe in it, then we should be striving to do what the Bible says. But you need to know for yourself. This really is God's Word, but you'll never make it a part of your life unless you firmly believe it is what it says it is. Put it to the test and you'll discover that it really is a firm place to put your faith.

How would you respond to someone who says the Bible is just another book?

Think about an experience you've had when you knew God spoke truth to you through the Bible.

Day 2
Hebrews 4:12

"God told me..." Have you ever heard people talk as if God speaks to them personally? Maybe you've wondered why God doesn't do that for you. To be honest, God doesn't tell me audible things either. But

God *is* talking to you. God speaks through his Word. This passage tells us the Bible doesn't just give us facts about God; rather, God uses it to help us in our present circumstances. In this chapter the author quotes some passages from the Old Testament and shows how God uses them to speak to those reading his letter. In the same way, the Holy Spirit will use these ancient texts to speak to you now. That's why reading the Word of God is so important.

What could God be trying to tell you through the verse you just read?

Do you ever expect God to speak to you while you're reading Scripture? Why or why not?

Day 3
Psalm 19:7-12

Why do we read the Bible and try to live by it? I believe most people assume we do so we can be more righteous. But verses 7 and 8 challenge that assumption. Look at all the benefits you get from living according to God's Word: It restores your soul, makes you wise, and brings joy to your heart. Following God doesn't just make you holy; it also makes you happy. David gave us the reason why he got up every day for his prayer time: It made his life work. That's what most people miss about righteousness: It's the best way to live the most joyful life imaginable. And that's what God wants for you, too. Reading and obeying the Bible each morning is a huge part of that.

Think about how living God's way can make your life work better.

Do you have a daily plan for reading and obeying God's Word?

Day 4
Matthew 4:1-11

We've all been tempted before—even Jesus. But look at how he responded in this situation. In each place where Satan tempted him, Jesus replied with Scripture. Remember, the Bible is living and active. There's power when you fight back, not with just your own opinion, but with the unchanging Word of God! A friend of mine at a secular college told me that people always respond differently when you quote Scripture in a discussion. It's one thing to talk as a person; it's another to speak the words that God wrote.

Do you know some verses you could use when you're tempted, or when you're sharing the gospel with someone? It's more powerful than you know.

Write down five verses you could quote right now.

What are some verses you need to memorize? As you read the Bible, ask God to show you some Scripture verses you should commit to memory.

Day 5
Psalm 119:9-16

Psalm 119 is the longest chapter in the Bible, topping out at 176 verses. (Don't worry; you don't have to read it all now.) The author wrote a stanza for each letter of the Hebrew alphabet. And every bit of it is about the Bible. Throughout the psalm the author talks about how knowing God's Word helps him to live, to be righteous, to honor God, and to live wisely. That's why he spent so much time thinking about it, meditating on it, and memorizing it. The Word of God was obviously a huge part of his life. Studying the Scriptures led to a passion for God's Word. The more you study the Word, the more you'll find this passion as well.

What place does the Bible have in your life?

Do you take it with you to school? Do you read it when you're not at church?

Are you studying it? The more you study God's Word, the more you'll be able to experience the joy that the psalmist described.

WEEK 27
PREACHING AND TEACHING: SECOND LETTER TO TIMOTHY (PART 2 OF 2)

MEMORY VERSE

"Don't let anyone look down on you because you are young, but set an example for the believers in speech, in life, in love, in faith and in purity." (1 Timothy 4:12)

INTRODUCTION

When you say the word *preaching*, images of ministers spitting out messages about hellfire and brimstone may come to mind. If it doesn't, then realize that for a lot of people in our culture, that's the only image of preaching they know. Examples of bad preaching are numerous: Televangelizing crooks, sandwich-board-wearing prophets, and finger-pointing bigots. But the preaching and teaching of the Church is much, much different. At the heart of the Church lies the gospel—the message of grace and new life through a relationship with Jesus.

God chose to reveal this message of hope to the world through you and me, followers of Christ. There's no Plan B. We're it! So the preaching and teaching of the Church is a top priority—not just for preachers, but for all of us. Paul knew this, and he wrote to young disciples, like Timothy, to make sure they understood the importance of the teaching of the Church. Paul wouldn't be around forever, so he made sure to pass on that message to others who could faithfully preach it to a new generation.

We need to make sure we're receiving good teaching and passing it on to others. Without the teaching of the Church, our beliefs would be reduced to the opinions of the latest charismatic leader.

The true message of the Church stands the test of time and isn't changed by the ideas of our culture. This week we'll look at why this is important and how we fit into the task of preaching and teaching today.

DAILY DEVOTIONS

Day 1
2 Timothy 4:1-5

"Uh, I'm not a minister." As a student that was my first reaction to this passage. Isn't Paul talking to a preacher? So what does this have to do with me? Realize that although Paul wrote this to Timothy, he meant for it to be read aloud to everyone in Timothy's church. And God apparently intended the same thing since he made sure Paul's letter to Timothy became a part of the Bible. Even those of us who aren't ministers have a responsibility to tell people about Jesus. Paul reminds us that our culture may one day stop listening, so we have to take every opportunity to preach and teach—no matter where it happens. Keep your eyes open for a chance to talk about your faith, to correct someone if they speak incorrectly about Christ, or to encourage someone with Scripture.

If God gave you an opportunity to talk about Christ today, what would you do?

Ask God to help you speak about him in some way today.

Day 2
Acts 4:1-4

Many people today say that if you believe something, then it's "true for you." As a result you can't tell people they're wrong. But this makes absolutely no sense. How can everyone be right all the time? The truth is they can't. Someone is right, and someone is wrong. Peter stood before the leaders of the Jewish faith claiming the only way to be saved is Jesus—the *only* way. One of the reasons we have to be serious about hearing good teaching is that a lot of people believe false things. There aren't 18 or 80 or 800 equally correct ways of living. There's only one. So it's important that we make sure we're right. By studying the Bible, listening to good teachers, and challenging bad teaching, we stay on track and avoid silly beliefs—such as whatever anyone believes is right "as long as they sincerely believe it."

Is learning the truth important to you, or do you listen only to those people who tell you what you want to hear?

Ask God to help you find the truth and show you any lies you're believing.

Day 3
Philippians 3:12-16

Have you ever read something in Scripture and thought, *I just don't understand*? Me, too. In fact it happens to everyone at times. Look at this passage. Paul knew that not everyone understood him at first. But he was confident that if his readers would keep working at it, then God would help them understand. Sometimes it takes time for us to grasp things; but don't worry, we're not on our own. Even if you don't feel very good at thinking about certain biblical things, remember that the Holy Spirit will help you understand everything you need to know. Our job is to make sure we don't give up after one try. Studying takes time. So don't get discouraged if it's hard at first. It does get easier. Keep at it!

How do you react when you don't understand something the first time?

Go back to a passage you found hard to comprehend and ask God to help you understand it. Spend time really thinking about it.

Day 4
1 Peter 2:1-3

Growing up is something you really don't have any control over. You go to bed one height and wake up two inches taller. Weird, I know. Spiritual growth doesn't work the same way, though. People don't automatically grow up spiritually. Some people become Christians but stay spiritual infants their whole lives. Can you imagine being a baby for 20, 30, or 40 years? Peter encourages his church to dig into Scripture because he knows that's the best way for believers to grow in their faith. Without the Word in our lives, we'll never be able to grow up to enjoy all the blessings of walking with God. Don't settle for being saved; that's just the beginning. Make it a habit to drink in God's Word. You'll be surprised at how much it helps you.

Is Scripture a chore or a blessing for you to read?

Ask God to give you a hunger for the Bible. Keep praying for that until it happens.

Day 5
Ephesians 6:10-18

Spiritual warfare is a reality. That doesn't mean you're going to have to speak weird prayers to cast horned demons out of your locker. But it does mean that invisible battles are happening around you daily. How do we get into the fight? Paul talks about arming ourselves with God, and then he speaks of a weapon: The sword of the Spirit. It's the only offensive weapon in the list. The Word of God is our weapon for attacking Satan's schemes and protecting ourselves. But you have to know it to use it. Reading the Bible, attending Bible studies, and doing what you're doing right now will help you learn how to use Scripture. Learning that skill is crucial to winning the spiritual battle we're all fighting.

Do you make time for Bible study each week?

How can you use what you're learning to help others?

WEEK 28
GOING TO MACEDONIA: PAUL'S VISION

MEMORY VERSE

"During the night Paul had a vision of a man of Macedonia standing and begging him, 'Come over to Macedonia and help us.' After Paul had seen the vision, we got ready at once to leave for Macedonia, concluding that God had called us to preach the gospel to them." (Acts 16:9-10)

INTRODUCTION

Wouldn't it be great if we had road signs for life, such as College, Turn Here or Character Work Next Four Months? They might not make life easier, but we'd be a little more confident about which choices to make. These signs would be helpful in our spiritual lives as well. But unfortunately, there are no such signs.

Some people believe following God is easy; it's usually anything but easy. One of the frustrating aspects of following God is that we often don't know where we're going. We may have one idea about how to serve God, only to discover God wants us to do something else. This can be frustrating and even discouraging if we're not careful.

So often we can see only the next step in our journey. And our limited perspective means we don't always know what's best for us. God, on the other hand, can see our entire journey. Therefore, when God asks us to make sacrifices or change our plans, it's always in our best interest to obey. The result honors God and brings us to the best possible place in our own lives.

Don't think you're alone in this. Even the apostles had experiences like ours. Acts 16 records a story of how Paul went through some frustrations before he finally discovered God's will concerning the next phase of his ministry. This week we're going to look at how Paul dealt with this change of plans and see what resulted. So put on your traveling shoes; we're about to make a detour.

DAILY DEVOTIONS

Day 1
Acts 16:6-10

Paul just wanted to preach. He was so passionate to see people saved that he'd have gone anywhere to share Jesus with them. But on occasion God had very specific plans for Paul and company. By pointing them to Macedonia (present-day Greece), the gospel penetrated Europe for the first time. Europe later became the center of Christianity for centuries. Of course Paul had no knowledge of this. He simply went where the Spirit led him. We won't always receive such specific guidance; but when we do, we should always heed it—even if we don't see the reason why. You probably already knew that. But then why do we rarely listen for God's direction?

Do you take time to regularly listen for the voice of God?

If God asked you to do something you didn't completely understand, would you trust God and do it anyway? Why or why not?

Day 2
Acts 16:11-15

Put yourself in Paul's shoes. All he wanted to do was tell people about Jesus. He even had a personal encounter with Jesus who told him to do just that. But for some reason, God wouldn't let Paul preach in the province of Asia. Paul had the right motive and the right mission, so what was the problem? Sometimes God's will just doesn't make sense to us. Sometimes God will ask us to forego something we really want, even when it's a godly request. This doesn't mean that God is angry or that what you requested is wrong. It just means God has a better plan in mind. We have to learn to trust God even when it doesn't make sense to us.

Has God ever denied a request you thought was godly?

How did you respond?

Ask God to give you the faith to obey even when the reasons aren't apparent.

Day 3
Jeremiah 20:7-9

As a young boy, Jeremiah was called to be a prophet. But fulfilling that calling was easier said than done. In fact Jeremiah lamented so much about the things he had to preach that he's now called "the weeping prophet." Why was it so hard for Jeremiah to do his job? Because no one listened to him. We live in a sinful world where God isn't honored universally. When we do our best to obey God, we'll almost always face opposition. But opposition doesn't mean you're off track. When you struggle for trying to live God's way, it typically means you're right where you need to be. Following God's will isn't always this hard, but it's not always easy, either. Don't judge your place in God's will by your circumstances or how you feel. Instead, trust God who called you in the first place.

What's been the hardest thing you've had to do to obey God?

Ask God for determination like Jeremiah's and the ability to obey God even when it's hard.

Day 4
Philippians 4:14-19

Remember, Paul didn't originally want to go to Europe. But he went there anyway because that's where God wanted him to go. Paul probably went there somewhat reluctantly, especially if he had his heart set on the province of Asia. But look at the results. Philippi was one of the first places where Paul planted a church. Not only did it become an amazingly healthy church, but it was also one of Paul's favorites. In today's passage we see how this church supported Paul when no other church would. You may find yourself having to give up something you love or enjoy for an uncertain future. Just like moving to a new town, it's hard to give up the good things you have for the good things you don't know about. But trust in God is always rewarded. Change is hard; but when God calls us to change, it will always lead to something better.

What would have happened if Paul hadn't obeyed God but had gone to the province of Asia instead?

Will you obey God even if it means giving up something you love or enjoy?

Day 5
Numbers 14:1-10

I wouldn't want Moses' job. Anytime there was a problem, the whole nation talked about going back to Egyptian slavery. Even here, on the verge of entering the Promised Land, the people didn't want to go because they were going to have to fight for it. These people would've settled for living in slavery or wandering in the desert instead of trusting God and moving forward. As silly as this seems, we do this all the time when we're not willing to follow God in faith. Faith by its very nature is difficult. But when we choose to follow God instead of the status quo, we'll find ourselves in the land flowing with milk and honey—not out in the cold.

Are there any areas of your life in which you don't want to follow God in faith? What are they?

Are you complacently settling for the present instead of trusting God with the future?

WEEK 29
SINGING IN JAIL: PAUL AND SILAS IN PRISON

MEMORY VERSE

"He then brought them out and asked, 'Sirs, what must I do to be saved?' They replied, 'Believe in the Lord Jesus, and you will be saved—you and your household.'" (Acts 16:30-31)

INTRODUCTION

Have you ever hit your funny bone? You know what I'm talking about, although I'm sure this isn't the technical name for it. Often when I hit my elbow, first I feel a shooting pain, but right after I also have a desire to laugh. My arm hurts, but it makes me laugh, too. It's weird how pain and laughter can coexist. It doesn't make sense, but it happens.

This week we're looking at an equally improbable event. Paul and Silas were beaten and thrown into prison, but then they led a worship service from their jail cell. How can someone experience such pain yet still sing? Our reaction to bad situations is one way we show a lost world that Christ is real. When we're able to see Christ in the midst of our pain, we find strength where others find only emptiness and despair.

Like Shadrach, Meshach, and Abednego, if we turn our troubles over to God, then we discover that God walks with us in the fire. And when we step out of the flames in one piece, everyone marvels at the fact that God provided help in our time of pain. God can help us become people who react like Paul and Silas did. The bad news is that it usually takes a lot of tough experiences to build that kind of character. But we have to start somewhere. And we don't have to do it alone.

DAILY DEVOTIONS

Day 1
Acts 16:16-34

They did what? How in the world do you find the ability to sing your favorite worship chorus when your back is on fire from your latest beating and you can't get to sleep because of the pain? Yet here they are, responding as Christ would. And that's really the key here. If you're saying to yourself, *I couldn't do that*, then you may be right. But how can you get to the point where you could? Not by trying really hard to sing whenever you hurt. These guys sang because that was the response that came out of them; it was their character. When we're really hard-pressed during difficult times, what's deep inside us will surface. Don't try to make it happen; ask God to change you so this will be your natural reaction.

How would you have responded in this situation?

Ask God to change who you are deep down, not just on the surface.

Day 2
2 Corinthians 1:3-7

Never forget this message from verse 3: Our God is the God of all comfort. No matter how you feel, this is God's nature; God longs to help us and to comfort us when we're hurting. Sometimes that help doesn't come in the way we want, but that doesn't change God's nature. When you go to God for help, God will provide. Period. But note that God wants to comfort us so we can then comfort others. When we've been through a rough time and find peace in the midst of strife, we're able to go to others who are still in the midst of the fight and show them they can survive with God's help—just like we did. When we do this, it causes us to love those who are hurting. As we comfort others, we're becoming more like Christ.

How has God been the God of all comfort to you?

How can you help those who are going through struggles similar to yours?

Day 3
2 Corinthians 1:8-11

If Paul had times in his life that made him think he was going to die, then I'm sure we'll have our own share of difficult days as well. Think about it: Paul was very close to God, but he still had moments in which he wondered what was going on. When you face harsh circumstances, it's normal to be afraid, to wonder where God is, and to hate the pain. But you still get to choose how you respond. Paul saw the bigger picture; he didn't need to rely on his own power—but on God's—to get through trials. It's easy to try to manage on our own, but God asks us to have faith in him, even in—*especially* in—the midst of our pain.

Think through your latest trial and note how you responded. Did you rely on God's power or your own?

Ask God to show you how to respond like Paul in the midst of pain.

Day 4
James 1:2-4

This is one of those verses that most of us just don't get. Why would anyone rejoice over hard times? James wasn't some sadistic person who thought we should enjoy pain. Instead, he reminds us to look beyond our circumstances to the fact that God is always using our problems for our ultimate good. Knowing that our struggles aren't in vain helps us to endure them a little easier. In fact this knowledge becomes a huge source of encouragement when we're hurting. Remember, nothing that happens to you is wasted. Even if Satan intends it for evil, God will turn it around for good. This bit of truth can't stop your pain, but it can help you find joy in spite of your pain.

How has God used past hurts to help you now?

Thank God for being present in the midst of your trials and for using them in ways you can't see...yet.

Day 5
Acts 16:25-30

Just as God never fails to use our trials for our good, God also uses our responses to turn a bad situation into a good one. The effect of Paul and Silas' responses to their torture was so stunning that even when the prison doors flew open, the other prisoners refused to leave. Imagine that! They'd rather stay in jail with the people who could find joy in a prison cell than return to their lives outside their cells. The jailer was so moved by what he saw that he became a Christian moments later. Our trials aren't just about us. When we see that God is using our trials to help others, it can give us the confidence to continue trusting God even though the pain is still real.

Ask God to show you how he's used your reactions to problems and trials to help others.

Try to look beyond your own pain and see how God can use you in the midst of it.

WEEK 30
A UNIFIED CHURCH: LETTER TO THE PHILIPPIANS

MEMORY VERSE

"Do nothing out of selfish ambition or vain conceit, but in humility consider others better than yourselves." (Philippians 2:3)

INTRODUCTION

It challenges me anytime I see a large group of people coming together for a common purpose. When this happens, it shows that something is more important than their differences—something that transcends personal ambitions.

God is trying to build that same spirit of unity in us. One of the things Paul stressed in the prison epistles of Philippians and Ephesians is the unity of the church. But how do such different people act in concert? By imitating Christ and following the example he set. What an incredible unified body we'd be if everyone in the church were to follow this example. One day this will be a reality, and we're all going to see it. But until then, God is busy building that unity among us.

We're going to take a look at the unity of the church and discover that God truly desires for us to put aside our differences and come together as one universal Church. It's going to require some changes on all our parts. But the result will be a sight that will do more than simply confound divisive politicians; it will change the whole world.

DAILY DEVOTIONS

Day 1
Philippians 2:1-4

Being one in purpose isn't the easiest thing to do. Most of us would prefer that everyone else agree with us. But Paul didn't just command the Philippians to be unified; he also told them their unity was a sign that they'd been changed. Like the Philippians, we were unable to experience true unity until Christ changed us. And now our unity is one of the signs that Jesus is moving in us. If we can't be unified with other believers, then our spirituality is in question. But if we've truly experienced Christ, then we should also be changed.

How do you interact with other believers? Can you get along with other Christians?

Is working with other believers a priority for you? The Holy Spirit will help you when this is hard.

Think on all the things mentioned in verse 1 and thank Christ for those gifts. Then pray that God would show you how to share those gifts with other believers today.

Day 2
Philippians 2:5-11

I like my life. More to the point, I like *how* I live my life: However I want to. But when you have a family or live with other people, you find out very quickly that you have to make some changes if everyone is going to get along. Compromise is necessary to make life work in community. Jesus thought it was worth the price. See all the things he had to do to bring us into the family? But he believed it was worth laying aside his glory—just for us. If Jesus was willing to do all of that for us, then we need to be willing to make sacrifices for others. It's not always easy (it certainly wasn't for Jesus), but it does bring about new life.

What areas of your life will you have to change in order to live in unity with other believers? Are you willing to make those sacrifices?

Ask God to show you how to do that through his power—not your own.

Day 3
John 17:20-23

How's this for a startling statement: Jesus prayed that, as believers, we'd have the same kind of unity that exists in God himself. He is Father, Son, and Holy Spirit, yet still one God. It's a mystery, to be sure, but that's the model for how unified he wants us to be. If we're able to live in that kind of unity, then it shows people that something supernatural is present. Disunity is natural—even expected (kind of like how you and your siblings sometimes get on each other's nerves).

So imagine how stunned people would be if Christians all lived in unity. It's possible through Christ, but only if we're willing.

If you feel you're not living in unity with other believers, then what's holding you back?

What are you doing to clear away the obstacles?

Ask God to enable you to overcome anything that would keep you from having this kind of intimacy with others.

Day 4
Revelation 7:9-10

Some people from certain denominations believe they'll be the only people in heaven; but I have a feeling heaven will be a bit more crowded than they expect. God's plan is for unity among all believers, but how do we unify all the different denominations? It's a lot of work to maintain unity in just one church, much less all churches. Is it really that big a deal? In this passage, we see the end of time. Here's a picture of the Church as God intends it to be, with believers from all over the world united and praising God together. If this is the plan, then we should already be working on our small part of that unity, as best we can.

Begin thinking about what it will look like for all of us to finally be worshiping together in heaven.

What's preventing you from working with believers from other denominations?

Day 5
Ephesians 4:1-6

One of the reasons it's hard to be unified with other believers is that we seem to be so different—different churches, different personalities, and even different opinions on minor issues. So how can we expect to get along? Paul reminds the Ephesians that while they do have a lot of differences, they also share a lot of similarities, which are much greater than their differences. We all have the same God, we were baptized into the same body of believers, and we have the same Holy Spirit. No matter who we are or what church we attend, if we're Christians, then we're all saved the same way: By the grace of God. No one deserves to be here more than anyone else because we all came through the same door. Once we recognize this fact, it's a lot harder to put up walls between us because, at our cores, we're all the same where it really counts: We're children of God.

What are some of the things that divide you from other believers?

Are they valid reasons for not being united?

WEEK 31
THE CHURCH EXPECTANT: THE RETURN OF CHRIST

MEMORY VERSE

"For to me, to live is Christ and to die is gain." (Philippians 1:21)

INTRODUCTION

As a kid, I could never sleep on Christmas Eve. I was too excited. Who knew what would be waiting for me under the tree when I got up? Would I get all the things I asked for? Expectation is a powerful force in our lives. It gives us hope, makes us excited, and helps us overcome obstacles and setbacks. But as believers, we aren't waiting for a present under a tree; we're waiting for the return of Christ!

As Paul traveled on his missionary journeys, he wrote to the churches he'd visited or helped start. These letters would eventually become many of the books of the New Testament. While on his second missionary journey, Paul wrote to the church in Thessalonica. Like a child on Christmas morning, the members of the church were anxious for the return of Christ. But they also had some questions, such as, "What happens to those people who died before Christ came to earth?" Paul answered their questions in 1 Thessalonians 4:13-18.

When Jesus comes again, everything will change. We'll get new bodies, we'll see our loved ones who have died, and we'll live forever with God. In the meantime God has given us a task to accomplish, and it may not always be an easy one. But if we keep our eyes focused on heaven, then we'll remember what we're fighting for. We should never settle for sin.

This week we'll look at the future of the Church and how that future helps us live here and now.

DAILY DEVOTIONS

Day 1

1 Thessalonians 4:13-18

A lot of people—Christians and non-Christians—wonder what life will be like in heaven. For example, will we remember our loved ones and will they remember us? Paul tells us in today's Scripture passage that when Jesus returns we'll all meet him in the air together. And though our bodies will be changed, our souls won't. So when we meet him, we'll still be who we are and our loved ones will be as well. That means they'll certainly remember us and vice versa. It's a reunion you don't want to miss!

Pray today for your non-Christian friends to turn to Jesus.

Look for opportunities to share Christ with them so they'll join you on the day of his return.

Day 2

Revelation 21:1-5; 21:22-22:5

We have a lot to look forward to! It's always great when God blesses us here on earth, but we need to remember that this isn't our home. Don't get too comfortable here because ultimately we're moving for good.

God is preparing something better for us and that's where we'll spend eternity. Eternity! In that place there will be no mourning or pain. So when we experience pain in this life, we need to always remember the future that's to come. It may be hard to be motivated by a place we've never seen; but as we dwell on our eternal destiny, it gives us the courage to face the pain we sometimes experience here.

Have you ever seriously thought about heaven? Spend some time trying to picture what heaven is like.

Thank God for preparing such an awesome place for us.

Day 3
1 Corinthians 15:50-56

People's number one fear is the fear of death, and rightly so. It ends all of what we've created for ourselves. Some people will do anything to get away from death. But for those of us who know we'll live forever with Christ, there's no need to worry. While thinking about death may make us a little uncomfortable, Christ has taken its ultimate effects away. So as Christians we can face death with dignity and expectation instead of fear. As Paul would later say: I can either stay here and serve Christ or go to be with him; either one is fine with me.
Are you afraid of death?

Spend some time with this passage and apply it to yourself.

Ask God to help you live without that fear.

Day 4
Acts 20:17-38

If we know we'll be reunited with our loved ones after death, then is it natural to mourn when they die? Of course it is. Jesus wept at the death of Lazarus even though Jesus knew he'd raise his friend from the dead a few moments later. In today's passage Paul's friends wept over him because they knew they wouldn't see him again before the resurrection. If we have real love for one another, then it's perfectly natural to mourn someone's passing. However, we don't mourn as the world mourns because we know this is just a brief separation; it's not permanent. We still cry, though, because we love the person. Mourning is a healthy part of dealing with death so we can move on with our lives.

Have you ever lost a loved one or a close friend?

Give yourself the freedom to mourn your loss, but always remember that if the person is a Christian, then you will see her again.

Day 5

2 Corinthians 5:6-8

Knowing we're heading home to be with Jesus helps us understand this statement: "We live by faith, not by sight." Faith in what? Faith that everything Christ says is real. We really will be raised from the dead. We really will live with him forever! When we know we have a future in heaven, and we'll be held accountable for all of our actions, we'll make better decisions here on earth. Unfortunately, many people live under a different philosophy: "Out of sight, out of mind." How you live is determined by which philosophy you choose. Remembering our heavenly home helps us stay on track and live as an expectant body of believers.

Which statement best describes how you actually live—"We live by faith, not by sight" or "Out of sight, out of mind"?

Ask God to give you a clear picture of your future and to help you live by faith—not by sight.

WEEK 32
THE UNKNOWN GOD: PAUL IN ATHENS

MEMORY VERSE

"For he has set a day when he will judge the world with justice by the man he has appointed. He has given proof of this to all men by raising him from the dead." (Acts 17:31)

INTRODUCTION

Imagine you get a chance to travel back in time and explore your favorite period of history. It sounds great at first, but then try explaining your world to the people living in that time. How would you describe electricity to someone from the Middle Ages? Those people would have a hard time understanding you because they have no frame of reference. Since they've never even imagined some of the things you're describing, they'd probably give you some funny looks.

In Acts 17:16-34 Paul found himself in a similar situation as he tried to explain Christ to the people in Athens, who had no frame of reference for a resurrected Messiah. While some people thought Paul was crazy, Paul got through to the Athenians by finding out what they knew and starting from there.

Witnessing to people isn't easy; but if we love them, then we'll do our best to paint a clear picture for them. There are people around you who have no idea what a personal relationship with Jesus is—or how to have one. And you may be the only person they know who can tell them. What will you say? Like Paul, this week we're going to figure out a game plan so we can meet people where they are and take the gospel to those who may have never heard Jesus' name.

DAILY DEVOTIONS

Day 1
Acts 17:16-34

How do you talk to people who don't even have a basic, foundational starting point for the God you want to talk about? One idea is to find something they *do* know and start from there. Witnessing isn't just about spouting recited lines to non-Christians. You can't ask people if they want to be "washed in the blood of the Lamb" if they don't know what you're talking about. They might believe you're a psychotic sheep rancher. Loving people means understanding them first and then explaining the love of Jesus in a way they can grasp. We must start where they are, not where we are. In today's verses Paul did that. He found some men who were very receptive. Before you start witnessing to people, find out more about them. Who are they? What are they like? It can make all the difference.

How would you begin to share Christ with someone who's never been to church?

Write out your testimony without using any church language (in other words, without using terms a non-Christian wouldn't understand).

Day 2
1 Corinthians 9:19-23

You can never put Paul in a box. As soon as you think you have him figured out, he'll surprise you. Why? Paul didn't think of himself all that much. Instead, he thought about the people who needed Christ and how best to reach them. He knew that one approach wouldn't reach everyone, so he decided to keep changing his approach to reach as many as possible. Reaching out means that we start with others, not ourselves. It means you ask yourself, *How can I explain Christ in a way they can hear and understand?* The answer will most likely be different for almost everyone you meet. But you'll also find you have a better audience for your message.

Are you willing to go into someone else's world in order to share the gospel with them—or do you ask them to come into yours?

What would you look like if you became "all things to all people"?

Day 3
Ecclesiastes 3:11; Acts 17:24-28

"But they're not going to listen to me!" How many times has this excuse kept you from sharing Christ with others? In this passage Paul is talking to people who are the complete opposite of the God-fearing Jews in the synagogue. Paul is confident they'll listen because although they're different, they're also human. God has put a longing within every person to seek God. Deep down everyone knows we're made to be more than mere mortals. So even though people look and sound different, God knows what's going on in their hearts. No matter whom you're talking to, you can always bank on this: Although they may not look like it, they may never tell you, and they may not even understand it themselves, everyone you know has a longing for God.

How does this knowledge change how you interpret the reactions of those you share Christ with?

Spend some time thinking about how your non-Christian friends are actually seeking eternal things—whether they know it or not.

Day 4
1 Peter 2:11-12

Saint Francis once said, "Preach the gospel; use words if necessary." When we reach out to those who don't know God, the first thing they evaluate is our behavior. In fact some may not even listen to our words until our behavior proves that we're different. Not everyone understands theology; but everyone can see that you're different when you love at times when others would hate, give at times when others would take, and pray at times when others would curse. Practical acts of love and service are surefire ways of opening doors to tell others why you live the way you live. Does it take longer? Sure, but it works. Does your lifestyle help or hurt your ability to share the gospel with others?

How can you live today in a way that preaches the gospel without words?

Day 5

1 Corinthians 2:1-5

Have you ever started witnessing to someone only to find yourself in a religious debate? It's frustrating and typically unproductive. We can usually avoid this kind of scene if we stay focused. If not, then we'll end up talking to people about the problems and consequences of sin without ever getting to the core issue: Their need for Christ. Confronting someone who cheats on his tests without addressing the need for Christ isn't enough; you point out sin (cheating) but won't cure the illness (sin nature).

Don't get sidetracked by secondary issues; instead, make sure the focus is on Jesus. His death on the cross is the answer for all of us. Let Jesus deal with all the issues in his time. We need to stay focused on Christ's life, death, and resurrection.

When you talk to others about Jesus, do you talk more about his rules or his salvation?

Ask Jesus to help you focus on him as you tell others about him today.

WEEK 33
A NIGHT'S VISION: PAUL IN CORINTH

MEMORY VERSE

"One night the Lord spoke to Paul in a vision: 'Do not be afraid; keep on speaking, do not be silent. For I am with you, and no one is going to attack and harm you, because I have many people in this city.'" (Acts 18:9-10)

INTRODUCTION

While I was on a mission trip to Mexico, some policemen rounded up a bunch of guys in our worship service and led them outside—they walked right past me. One policeman told me they were some local gang members causing trouble. I asked if they could stay, but I was ignored. *Too bad*, I thought. *I wish they could have heard the gospel.* Suddenly I felt God leading me to tell these guys about Jesus. My response to God was that talking to gang members was not my spiritual gift. God didn't buy it. So, scared to death, I went to the parking lot to chase down 12 gang members and tell them about Christ.

My situation was a cakewalk compared to what Paul endured. As he traveled on his missionary journeys, people routinely wanted to kill him. This always makes me wonder if Paul ever got scared. The answer must be "yes," since in Acts 18 Paul received a special vision from God reminding Paul that God would always be with him. Armed with that confidence, Paul never wavered as he preached and taught.

God may ask us to do things that are frightening, but he'll always be with us. And while our fear may not go away completely, we can have faith in God that he won't let us down. This week we'll look at how to find courage in the midst of difficult ministry moments.

DAILY DEVOTIONS

Day 1
Acts 18:9-17

Paul wasn't paranoid; people really were trying to kill him. It's one thing to tell others about Jesus. It's quite another to tell people about God when they may want to kill you afterward. God reassured Paul that he'd be protected. God kept this promise. When the Jews tried to get Paul beaten by the Romans, the Romans didn't find him guilty. In fact the only one who was beaten that day was one of Paul's accusers. God promises in Scripture to help us stand firm in the face of opposition. This passage proves that as we obey God, God will do what God promises.

What are some areas of your life in which you're tempted to back down from doing what you know you need to do?

Which of God's promises do you rely on to avoid those temptations? Write them here—or find some in Scripture.

Day 2
Jeremiah 9:23-24

Strength and confidence come from many places. Some people are confident because they're popular, wealthy, or talented. But none of these things is stable enough to be relied upon. We need to always be on guard against false pride. We may feel we're walking tall with God, but where does that confidence come from? Is it because we really know God or because we simply look good to others? In order to walk in courage and humility, we must develop a real relationship with God, not just go through the motions. Any other type of confidence will ultimately fail us. Remember, there's nothing more important than your personal walk with God.

Where does your confidence come from?

How can you gain real confidence?

What do you learn about God from this passage?

Spend some time talking to God about these attributes.

Day 3
Joshua 1:1-9

Imagine you've just been handed the leadership over a million people. Now you're about to go start a war with 10 other nations, and you have no idea what you're doing. No pressure, right? No wonder God gave this advice to young Joshua: Don't fear!

Since we're being asked to do something we can't do on our own, having faith and moving forward are always accompanied by at least *some* fear. But we can never let fear keep us from being faithful. This is courage: Choosing to obey even when we're uncertain. Following

Christ demands courage even if you have a little less responsibility than Joshua did. No one said this would be easy, but God promises to be with us every step of the way.

God gives Joshua two commands and a promise in this passage. What are they?

How are you obeying these same commands that were given to Joshua?

Day 4
Acts 18:11; 19:10; 20:31

Paul was no fly-by-night preacher. He knew that in order to have an effective ministry, he couldn't just preach a sermon and expect that to fix all the problems. So he stayed in certain towns for months and even years. But the real fruits of his labors were the churches that lasted for decades and centuries. Sometimes the hard part of ministry is sticking with it. The temptation to quit may not come from a physical threat, but from the day-to-day exhaustion of keeping up. The courageous thing is to keep going. And courage sometimes means refusing to quit and seeing God's will through to the end.

Have you ever just wanted to quit being faithful?

How can the results of Paul's ministry encourage you to persevere?

Ask God for the strength to continue when you have no strength left.

Day 5
2 Timothy 2:1

At one time this was a confusing verse to me. How can grace make you strong? If I need grace, then doesn't that mean I need help? So how can needing help make me strong? Paul wasn't protected because he worked harder or was holier than others. He was protected because God loved him. We don't need to be strong in our own abilities, but rather strong in God's amazing and unfailing love for us. No matter who you are or what you've done, if you're a believer, then you can be strong in God's grace instead of trying to do things on your own. And I guarantee it's easier to live in the grace of God than trying to live life solo.

What would it look like for you to be strong in the grace of Jesus Christ?

Ask God for help to live in his grace and not in our own abilities.

WEEK 34
INTERNAL DIVISIONS: FIRST LETTER TO THE CORINTHIANS (PART 1 OF 4)

MEMORY VERSE

"Live in harmony with one another. Do not be proud, but be willing to associate with people of low position. Do not be conceited." (Romans 12:16)

INTRODUCTION

Have you ever felt betrayed—like when you found out your best friend was talking about you behind your back? It's worse—much worse—than finding out your worst enemy is trashing you. We expect that kind of treatment from our enemies but not from our friends. As Christians I believe we're ready to fight spiritual forces that are set against us and even people who don't believe in Christ. But it's a shock to realize you'll often end up fighting other people in your church.

Paul experienced this firsthand. While on his third missionary journey, in Ephesus, Paul wrote to the church in Corinth. After wading through angry mobs of pagans in town after town, Paul found out that the believers in Corinth were fighting amongst themselves. The same thing happens today. Almost all of us know of a church that's split over some trivial matter like the color of the carpet. What's going on? Satan will never fight fair. If he can sabotage churches, then he's more than willing to do so.

This week we'll look at some internal problems that cropped up in the New Testament Church and see how God wants us to deal with them today. Any conflict can be defeated when we allow Christ and his truth—not our prideful opinions—to be our guide.

DAILY DEVOTIONS

Day 1
1 Corinthians 3:1-9

Most of us like to believe we're more mature than we actually are. Like the time you told your parents you were so ready to drive—at age 13! At times like that, we need a reality check, which is exactly what Paul gave the Corinthians here. For all their lofty opinions of themselves, Paul told them he couldn't teach them the really deep parts of the faith because they wouldn't get it. In effect he said, "Telling you deep things is like trying to explain physics to an eight-year-old; you just aren't mature enough to understand it." The Corinthians were capable of maturing so they could hear those things; they just thought they were already mature when they really weren't. That kind of pride is costly.

Take an honest inventory of your spiritual life. Are you an infant or are you growing steadily?

Ask God to help you grow day by day so you won't miss out on anything you're supposed to learn.

Day 2
2 Corinthians 11

Whoa! How's that for a tirade? If you've never read sarcasm in the Bible, then here it is.

It seems odd for us, but Paul was actually defending his status as an apostle. Other "super teachers" were trying to put Paul down, saying he wasn't flashy enough and he didn't act like the other charlatans who were running around. Translation for today: Paul wasn't cool/funny/popular enough. But Paul made no apologies for this. He was more interested in telling people the truth than tickling their ears. We have to be very careful about whom we listen to; otherwise, we'll end up like the Corinthians who started dismissing Paul—Paul!—for some other guy who made them laugh. We've got to be on guard against flashy hypocrites, no matter how cool they seem.

Whom do you follow as a spiritual leader? Why?

Ask God to show you who true spiritual leaders are and how to spot impostors before they lead you astray.

Day 3
Philippians 4:2-3

I know this never happens in your church; but apparently in the Philippian church, some women weren't getting along. Disagreements are a common—yet costly—problem. When people hold grudges, get angry, or refuse to compromise, they end up spending precious time and energy putting out relational fires instead of focusing on the work God has for them. Satan can't destroy the church, but he can sidetrack us. Prompting fights between church members is an easy way for him to accomplish that. So if you find yourself in a disagreement with someone at church, make every effort possible to resolve the situation quickly by practicing patience and forgiveness. I know that's easier said than done, but it's more important than you know. And we can't afford to put off the work of God.

Are you in a situation like these two women? Why can't it be resolved today?

Spend some time praying for wisdom, patience, and a spirit of forgiveness.

Day 4
1 Corinthians 1:8

The Corinthian church had a lot of issues that Paul tried to tackle. That's probably why 1 Corinthians is such a long letter. One of the main issues was that the Corinthians thought they knew it all, and their pride led them to hurt each other. They started to focus on minor things (like being able to eat whatever they wanted) instead of major things (like loving their fellow church members). Paul told them to get off their pedestals and see what was happening. I don't believe anyone does it on purpose, but we can drift in a prideful direction if we're not careful.

Are there any ways in which you believe you're more spiritual than most?

Ask God to reveal any places where your pride is causing you or others to stumble.

Day 5
Romans 12:17

It's a sad reality that people hurt us occasionally—intentionally or unintentionally. We don't have any control over that, but we do have control over our responses. Paul reminds us to react as Jesus did, and he even gives us a reason why: God will ultimately deal with all wrongs. So we don't have to get revenge; God will deal justly with everyone. God's answer when we get hurt isn't, "Get over it"; it's "I'll take care of it. Just trust me." Knowing that, it's easier for us to allow God to resolve situations instead of addressing them ourselves.

Are you refusing to live at peace with someone?

According to this Scripture, what should you do?

Ask God to help you give him control of the difficult situations of your life.

WEEK 35
ACCOUNTABILITY: FIRST LETTER TO THE CORINTHIANS (PART 2 OF 4)

MEMORY VERSE

"Brothers, if someone is caught in a sin, you who are spiritual should restore him gently. But watch yourself, or you also may be tempted." (Galatians 6:1)

INTRODUCTION

I never would've survived high school without my best friends. Together we had some of the best years of our lives, but we also kept each other from straying away from Christ. We were accountable to one another.

In Week 9 we figured out that if we're going to have integrity as a church, then we can't let sin go unchecked. That's easy enough when we're the problem, but it gets a little harder when we have to tell someone else what they're doing is wrong. That's where accountability comes in.

As Paul planted churches, he didn't forget about them once he left. While he traveled, he routinely kept track of them and even made return visits to make sure they stayed healthy. So when Paul found out the Corinthians were allowing sin to go unchecked, he wrote a letter to keep them accountable to their commitment to Christ.

Every now and then we'll have friends who stray off the path. When that happens, we need to be there to help them get back on the right track, just like we'll need them to help us. I know it sounds unpleasant, and it can get messy. But when we actually start holding each other accountable, you'll be surprised how much it helps your own spiritual life. Instead of dealing with sin on your own, you can tackle it with the help of your Christian friends. But it starts when we're honest about our own lives and open to listening to others when they confront us.

Ready? Let's figure out how we can hold each other accountable this week.

DAILY DEVOTIONS

Day 1
1 Corinthians 5:1-13

Sin is serious; but apparently the Corinthians had forgotten that fact. Paul was furious. The church had failed to see the danger in allowing a sinful activity to go unchecked. So now Paul demanded they stop allowing such behavior. He told them to exclude the immoral person from the church. This "handing over to Satan" would hopefully help this person see that his actions were incompatible with godly living and prompt him to repent and return. Sound too harsh? Remember, sin is serious. But the goal was not to have him remain outside. Paul's love was tough love, but it was love in its truest form, a love that wouldn't allow a friend to destroy himself.

Do you know a Christian who is consistently living in an ungodly way?

How would Paul suggest you deal with this person? Are you living in a way that's consistently ungodly? What can you do to address your sinful actions?

Day 2
Matthew 18:15-20

It would be great if we all figured out everything on the first try, but it usually doesn't work that way. Sometimes we must confront our friends. Jesus knew this was complicated, so he set guidelines for how to confront fellow believers when they sin. Keeping the situation between the two of you is best. If the situation can be resolved without involving other people, then it will prevent gossip and other issues. But if your friend resists listening to you, then try taking one or two others along for a chat. If that doesn't work, then as a last resort the whole church should be informed and the church leadership should be involved. These guidelines not only protect the person being confronted, but they keep us in check as well.

Have you ever had to confront someone about a sin you noticed in his life? How did it go?

Did you use these guidelines from Matthew? If not, then would these guidelines have helped?

Pray for the patience to humbly walk with someone if God calls you to a confrontation.

Day 3
Psalm 141:3-5

Now here's an odd scene. David was actually praying that his friends would punch him and tell him he was wrong. What's going on here?

David had already figured out that he preferred to do the wrong thing at times. (Can you relate?) On some occasions he deliberately committed a sin and paid the price. The other thing he knew was that he had friends who would tell him the truth. But no one wants to be told they're wrong. So he made a commitment to listen to his friends when they held him accountable. Your truest friends are those who will love you enough to let you know when you're wrong. You may need them more than you know. If David needed accountability, then I'm pretty sure we do, too.

Do you have friends who love you enough to tell you you're wrong?

Do you love your friends enough to help them see when they're sinning and hurting themselves?

Ask God to provide those kinds of friends for you and help you to be that kind of friend as well.

Day 4
Matthew 7:1-5

Have you ever met someone who loved to point out your faults but would never acknowledge he'd done anything wrong? Accountability is important, but we need to remember that God has not called us to be everyone's watchdog. God calls us to help each other get through sin, but first we need to recognize where we're failing. Checking yourself before you confront someone helps you in two ways. First, it helps you sympathize with someone as a fellow sinner. Next, it protects you from pridefully believing you're better than the other person. People are much more willing to listen when they feel understood.

All of us have sinned; does that mean we shouldn't confront others when they sin? What does the passage say?

Ask God to keep you humble—but firm—as you interact with others.

Day 5
Galatians 6:1-5

When I think about accountability, I think about telling someone he's wrong. But Paul knew it was much more than that. He describes accountability as helping carry each other's burdens. If we're really helping each other in love, then we're not just concerned with telling someone their faults. Instead, we're willing to help them walk out of that bad situation. This is what real love looks like. If we're not willing to help someone walk the hard road out of sin, then we may not be ready to confront that person. Real accountability is a long-term process, not a one-time reprimand. This is what Christ does for us—and it's what he's calling us to do for others.

Think about some ways you can carry your friends' burdens today.

WEEK 36
COMMUNION: FIRST LETTER TO THE CORINTHIANS (PART 3 OF 4)

MEMORY VERSE

"God has raised this Jesus to life, and we are all witnesses of the fact."
(Acts 2:32)

INTRODUCTION

Little cups filled with grape juice. Little pieces of bland bread. Must be communion time again. We've all probably participated in communion, but do we actually understand what's going on? In the early Roman world, some people feared Christians since one of their rituals supposedly included cannibalism—at least that's what some people *thought* was going on. They'd heard that to be a Christian you had to eat the body and drink the blood of Jesus. I guess to an outsider it does sound strange, but communion is an intimate and precious thing to a Christian.

Jesus asked us to regularly take part in communion. It's a continual reminder of Christ's sacrifice and constant union with us. If we don't keep this in mind, then we could miss out on the spiritual impact that communion can bring. Paul taught the churches to practice communion, but he had harsh words for those who failed to approach the communion table properly (for example, the Corinthians).

Does communion make sense to you? It's one of the church's most intensely personal traditions. This week we're going to spend some time looking at what happens when we take communion. Why did Jesus tell us to keep doing it? What's it about anyway? Look deep this week; there may be much more going on than you've ever imagined.

DAILY DEVOTIONS

Day 1
1 Corinthians 11:17-29

Yes, people actually got drunk at communion. Crazy, I know, but it's true. Jesus started communion with his disciples all together, not individually. The Corinthians had missed this, and they were being selfish during communion and ignoring some of the people they didn't like as much. But communion isn't just about your relationship with God, it's about all of us. God means for us to take communion together as a church family. When we do so, we're being united to Christ and to each other. So when you take communion, examine your relationship with God and your relationships with others in the church. If these aren't right, then make them right. Otherwise, you're missing the point—just like the Corinthians did.

Do you ever think about others during communion?

Ask God to show you ways you can become more united to your church family today.

Day 2
Luke 22:14-20

This story may seem all too familiar to us. Even the setting is familiar: A meal with friends. We probably eat with our friends all the time.

No big deal, right? Actually, this was a very special thing. In Jewish culture to share a meal was an intimate event. To invite someone to a meal was to say, "You're one of the closest people in my life." At his last meal, Jesus didn't offer a review of his teachings; he reminded the disciples that they were his friends. So when we take communion, realize that it's not just a ritual. God is literally inviting us into the deepest of friendships. God wants to be united with us, so he invites us to his table.

Do you have a close relationship with God or is it more distant? Why?

Imagine what it was like to be part of the communion at the Last Supper.

Day 3
Luke 18:31-33; 22:19

Let's take some time to dwell on the body of Christ. When Jesus broke the bread at the Last Supper, he knew that in the next few hours he'd be severely beaten and tortured. He knew what was coming, and he still offered his body to be broken for us. Think about the immensity of that sacrifice. If you knew you were facing physical harm, not to mention torture, then you'd probably avoid the situation. Jesus didn't. Instead, he walked into it on purpose, knowing it would cost his very life. He loves you that much. So when we take the bread, we need to remember the magnitude of the sacrifice Jesus made by offering his body to be broken for us.

Spend some time just thinking about what it would take to purposefully offer yourself for someone else.

Thank Jesus for his sacrifice for you.

Day 4
Luke 22:20; Hebrews 12:4

Today, let's dwell on the blood of Christ. Again, think about what it was like for Jesus at the Last Supper. He passed the cup knowing that in just a few hours, he'd see his own blood splattered on the ground. He knew that scourging (or whipping) and crucifixion were coming—both excruciatingly painful, bloody affairs. Now read Hebrews 12:4. The author reminds us that our struggles aren't nearly as hard as what Jesus did when he offered his blood for us. His love is that immense; his resolve that firm. So when you look at the cup during communion, realize that Jesus was giving his blood for you—on purpose—so that you could live and have eternal life.

Day 5
1 Corinthians 11:26

Communion may seem outdated to you. Maybe you've done it so often that it's lost its meaning. But Jesus meant for communion to be a living reminder for us—not only of what happened, but also of what's to come. Jesus died on the cross to show you how much he loved you, but he also did it to make sure you'd live with him forever. This story isn't over; he's coming back for us! When we take communion, we need to remember that the Savior who gave us his body and blood will come back to give us a new body as well.

When was the last time you thought about Jesus' return?

Try to live today remembering that Jesus is coming back soon. See what changes in your attitude.

WEEK 37
SPIRITUAL GIFTS: FIRST LETTER TO THE CORINTHIANS (PART 4 OF 4)

MEMORY VERSE

"All these are the work of one and the same Spirit, and he gives them to each one, just as he determines." (1 Corinthians 12:11)

INTRODUCTION

Maybe it's been a while since you put a puzzle together, but have you ever really studied a puzzle's pieces? They look like something out of a Picasso painting with their multiple legs, odd-shaped curves, and no hard edges (except for those blessed border pieces). No pieces seem identical. They all have a unique place to fill in the big picture, and the portrait won't be complete until every last one of them is in place.

God's Church is made in much the same way—as a puzzle. When you become a part of the Church, you receive a spiritual gift of some kind. One person may be given the ability to lead, another the ability to encourage, and still another the ability to make people feel welcome. No matter who you are, everyone gets a gift.

The Church functions like it's supposed to when all of us, like puzzle pieces, fit together and do our parts. Leave a piece out, and it's just not the same. Because you have this gift, you're a very important— even indispensable—part of the Church. Paul made this a top concern when he was teaching his churches so they'd understand that no one can walk alone. Churches aren't filled with spectators but with unique Christians, each with a role to play in the spiritual masterpiece of the Church.

This week we're going to look at what spiritual gifts are and how to determine which gifts you have.

DAILY DEVOTIONS

Day 1
1 Corinthians 12:4-11

I know it's better to give than to receive, but I still like getting gifts. In fact I'll take a gift pretty much any day of the week. Why? Gifts are for me, right? Well, on birthdays, yes; but in the church, no. God has given you a particular gift on purpose, but not just for your own personal benefit. God gave you a spiritual gift so you could use it to help others in the church, as well as yourself. Think about it. Healing, teaching, evangelism—none of these spiritual gifts works properly unless they're directed at others. So if we're going to get the most out of our spiritual gift, then we've got to be committed to serve others in the church with it. That's what your gift is for.

How does this thought change how you see your spiritual gift?

How does God want you to use your particular gift to help your church?

Day 2
1 Peter 4:10-11

Maybe you've never thought about your gift, or maybe you've wondered whether you even have one. "Sure, pastors have them; but what about me?" Notice in today's Scripture passage that Peter assumes everyone has a spiritual gift. If you're a Christian, then it's not possible for you *not* to have one. Peter told the people to use their gifts because he knew God had given gifts to each one of them; that's how the church works. If that's true, then we should spend some time trying to figure out what our gifts are. Your gift may not jump right out at you, but it also won't be the hardest thing in the world to discover.

Do you know what your spiritual gift is? What is it?

How do you know?

If you aren't sure what your gift is, ask God to help you discover it.

Day 3
Romans 12:6-8

Yesterday we figured out that we each have a spiritual gift; now we need to find out what it is. (Notice that Paul—like Peter—assumes we all have a gift.) In three separate passages, Paul lists about 20 gifts. So if you don't see yours in this particular list, that's okay. (See 1 Corinthians 12:8-10, 28 for some more possibilities.) Depending on your age, it may take some time for your gift to display itself, but that shouldn't stop you from trying to find out what it is. What things do you love to do most at your church? What things bring you the most joy as a believer? Don't know yet? Then try some things. Figuring this out may take some trial and error, so don't be afraid to jump in and see if something works for you.

Pick a gift you believe you might have and try using it this week.

Ask God for discernment to figure out what your gift is.

Day 4
1 Corinthians 13

Sometimes we believe our gifts are the most important, and we forget why we have them in the first place. That's what happened in Corinth. The Corinthians spoke in tongues—a lot. This was fine, but they'd missed the point of why they were given that gift. Here, Paul reminds them that their great knowledge and their ecstatic speech were useful only if they stemmed from a love for other people. If they didn't have that, then all the speaking in tongues and all the knowledge in the world was useless. Your gift is special, but it's given to you to love others.

According to today's passage, what's the foundation for all spiritual gifts?

Ask the Holy Spirit to help you love the people in your church more deeply this week.

Day 5
Romans 12:4-5

Back when I was younger, my family had strings with what seemed like hundreds of Christmas lights on them. The problem was that if you pulled just one light out of the string, then the rest of the lights wouldn't work. If there were 99 perfectly good lights and just one was defective, then the whole string didn't work. It was very frustrating! But the church is much the same. Whether you like it or not, you need all those other folks in your church. Each of them has a gift you need in order to make your gift work. If you don't use your gift, then everyone else suffers. And your gift won't work correctly unless it's connected to all the other gifts. This means there can be no loners in God's family. So it's important that we not only use our gifts, but also help others discover and use theirs. Doing so helps all of us.

How can you help your friends discover their spiritual gifts?

Pray today about how you can use your gift in connection with others at your church.

WEEK 38
GIVING: PAUL'S INSTRUCTIONS TO THE CORINTHIAN CHURCH

MEMORY VERSE

"Each man should give what he has decided in his heart to give, not reluctantly or under compulsion, for God loves a cheerful giver." (2 Corinthians 9:7)

INTRODUCTION

Bono, lead singer of the band U2, once said during a song, "The God I believe in isn't short of cash." He was criticizing phony TV preachers for stealing money from unsuspecting people. Lots of people have the same feeling. I meet people all the time who assume the only thing the church is after is their money. But Bono brings up a good point: If God can bless everyone, then why do we have to give—to God or to anyone else for that matter? Can't God just bless people? The answer is that it's not about the money.

We've received so much from God, it's only right that we honor him by giving some of it back. And as we give our resources away, it reminds us that the God who gave them to us in the first place will provide what we need. From cover to cover, the Bible records how people honored God by giving back to him. And we can still do this today through our local churches.

The early churches exemplified this concept of giving back to God by giving their money to help other churches that were in trouble. Paul not only taught his churches about giving, but he also gave them an opportunity to give an offering that he personally delivered to the Jerusalem church.

The generosity of the early churches is an example we follow today. This week we're going to look at why we need to give God our time, energy, and money.

DAILY DEVOTIONS

Day 1
2 Corinthians 9:6-15

It's not always easy to give our money away. We work hard to earn it, and we need it to buy necessities (and maybe some fun things as well). But in this passage, Paul reminds us why it can be easy: God is the great Provider. God owns everything, and God is always able to provide for you as you provide for others. No matter how much you give, God can always outgive you. So it all comes down to a question of trust. Do you really believe God can provide for you? A very easy way to check is to examine where your money goes.

Why is it so hard to give sometimes?

Think about some ways God is already providing for you. Ask God for faith to trust him in the areas of your life in which you're still holding on to your money.

Day 2
Luke 16:10-13

You should see a capital M on the word *money* in today's text. Jesus reminds us that our money can be very powerful spiritually—so much so, in fact, that Jesus refers to it as a god. If we aren't careful, then money will use us, instead of our using it. And it doesn't matter how much money you have, either. Don't believe me? Try giving away some of your money today and see what feelings immediately come to the surface. You might be surprised by how much of a hold it has on you. That's why Jesus tells us that it's important to learn how to use our money well in this life.

How does money affect you? Do you think about it a lot or a little?

Ask God to show you how to keep money in its proper place in your life.

Day 3
Malachi 3:8-10

Most of us assume that when the paycheck or allowance rolls our way, it's ours to do with however we see fit. But God makes a startling claim. Since the Israelites weren't giving God the full tithe, God says they were robbing him. God owns everything and gives generously to each of us. All God asks is that we acknowledge him by returning a portion of it and remembering that God will always provide for our needs. To not return a tithe, then, is to literally rob God of what he's due and deny that God gave it to us in the first place. Tithing isn't about your church or your money as much as it is about your relationship with God.

Do you tithe? Why or why not?

How would it change the way you live if you considered everything to be God's first and yours second?

Day 4
Malachi 3:8-10

God made a startling statement when he basically said, "Try me and just see if I won't come through—and come through in a big way!" God isn't opposed to wealth or to giving great blessings. When we're committed to God and give in faith, God is faithful to provide richly for us—and not necessarily with more money in our pockets. Remember, the point isn't giving in order to receive blessings; it's living in faith that God is in control and will always provide for us. When we believe this—and live it out—it's easy for God to bless us because he knows we'll use those blessings well.

We ask for a lot from God. How much do you give to God?

What are some ways you can trust God with your money this week?

Day 5

2 Corinthians 9:6-15

Let's end where we began this week. Why do we have to give to the church? It's an honest question. Some people say they'd rather give to a charity or to people they know. And that's fine. God wants us to give where there are needs. But giving to the church is different. When you give to the church, some very good things happen with your money. First, you're supporting the people God has put in your life to train you. And second, you're supporting all of the church's efforts to reach out to others, fund missionaries, help those in need, and provide for all sorts of activities to accomplish those goals. We're a part of a body, so when we give to church, we're actually taking care of God's people and God's plan to reach the world.

Is giving to your church a priority for you?

Talk to your pastor or church treasurer and ask how the church's money is spent.

WEEK 39
SPIRITUAL OPPOSITION: THE RIOT IN EPHESUS AND PAUL'S THIRD MISSIONARY JOURNEY

MEMORY VERSE

"Be self-controlled and alert. Your enemy the devil prowls around like a roaring lion looking for someone to devour." (1 Peter 5:8)

INTRODUCTION

Whenever I think of demons, those stone gargoyles found on old buildings come to mind. They have big fangs and ugly faces, but they're definitely stone. It's kind of hard to think of something like that as being a real threat in my life. Isn't a belief in demons about as outdated as the buildings where those gargoyles sit? Surprisingly, no. Demons are real, and they take every opportunity to stand in your way spiritually.

In Acts 19:21-41 Paul and his fellow travelers faced some pretty significant opposition. But look closer. The real reason behind the opposition was spiritual; these people were worshipers of a false god. They wanted nothing more than to be rid of Paul and his companions— by any means necessary.

You may not have to deal with physical opposition, but you'll definitely have to deal with spiritual warfare. You're in for it whether you like it or not. But how do you fight an invisible enemy, and what do spiritual battles feel like?

This week we're going to look at the invisible war Christians fight and hopefully find answers to some of your questions. Try to see beyond the visible this week and recognize what's really happening in the spiritual realm.

DAILY DEVOTIONS

Day 1
Acts 19:21-41; Ephesians 6:12

This was another close shave for Paul, but look at how he interpreted it. When he writes to the Ephesians afterward, he doesn't warn them against the men who tried to kill him, even though they're still around. Instead, he warns them about the spiritual forces that were behind the attack in the first place. Paul knew where the real threat lay: In the spiritual forces of darkness. Now don't get weird about it. You don't have to worry about demons leaping out at you from every corner. ("My car won't start—it must be a demon!") But our spiritual enemies are very real. Do you believe they just decided to quit after Jesus ascended to heaven? If they harassed him, then they'll harass us, too.

How does knowing you'll face spiritual opposition change your outlook toward being a Christian?

Day 2
Ephesians 6:13-19

This is one of those passages that everyone knows—but what do we do with it? Is there some sort of spiritual kung fu we can learn? Well, no, but that's not really necessary anyway. Look at the items that make up the armor. Each one is something we use on a daily basis (or at least we should): Faith, righteousness, truth. Fighting spiritual battles has less to do with praying unusual spiritual prayers ("Demon, come out!") and much more to do with living an authentic Christian life day in and day out. Using your faith, being prepared to share the gospel, and knowing God's Word are real weapons that will bring about real results in whatever spiritual battles you face.

What are some spiritual battles you're fighting?

How can you use your spiritual armor to fight those battles? Be specific—then go try these strategies.

Day 3
2 Corinthians 10:3-7

The Corinthians thought Paul was all bark and no bite. (He apparently wasn't all that intimidating to look at.) Paul reminds them, however, that not everything is the way it seems. He may not have looked powerful, but Paul's power came from God—and his weapons were more powerful than you can imagine.

Never underestimate the invisible war we're waging, but don't underestimate the power you have in Christ to fight it, either. Paul tells us to take every thought captive and make it obedient to Christ. So as you go through your day, be aware of the spiritual things going on and don't be afraid to jump in and stand up for God's truth.

Read today's Scripture passage again. How can you accomplish these tasks in your daily life?

Ask God to show you the places where you can take your thoughts captive for him today.

Day 4
1 Peter 5:8-9

Have you ever noticed that you deal with temptation more often when you're alone than when you're with other people? One of Satan's main tactics is to attack us when we're the weakest, which is typically when we're alone. A teacher once told me that we'll have a harder time overcoming temptation when we're hungry, angry, lonely, or tired—and she was right. Therefore, Peter tells us to be alert; he knows Satan is looking for someone to devour (not some group). Since Satan is always looking for a weak moment, we need to be aware of times when we're the most vulnerable. Don't let him surprise you. Instead, make sure you've always got good Christian friends you can hang out with or call when you feel tempted. Everyone needs that kind of help.

What do you struggle with the most when you're alone?

Have you ever told anyone about it? Why or why not?

Ask God to help you see temptations before they become unmanageable.

Day 5
Philippians 4:8-9

Most battles for the heart begin in the mind. For example, before you actually commit a sin, a battle is fought in your mind over whether or not you will. And it's here that the spiritual warfare gets thick. A lot of what goes into our minds, or what we choose to dwell on, actually pushes us toward sin instead of pulling us away from it. So being aware of what's going on in our minds is crucial if we want to win the battle against sin. Why? It's always easier to win a battle in your mind than to try to get out of a tough situation. If you overcome bad thoughts before they turn into bad actions, then you'll find yourself winning every time. Maybe it's time you shifted the battlefield to your mind.

Does your thought life resemble the verses you read today?

Spend some time choosing to reject thoughts that lead you away from the qualities in these verses—then watch to see if temptations are easier to handle.

WEEK 40
FAITHFULNESS AT GREAT COST: PAUL'S PARTING MESSAGE TO THE EPHESIANS

MEMORY VERSE

"Have nothing to do with godless myths and old wives' tales; rather, train yourself to be godly." (1 Timothy 4:7)

INTRODUCTION

I know of a youth group in which the students were in the habit of becoming very emotional during their Wednesday night service. Being emotional isn't wrong, but they seemed to get emotional for no reason. The youth minister decided to test them. So he preached an impassioned talk and then asked if any of them wanted to come forward and accept Christ. The altar area was full of students! Suddenly he stopped the service and informed the teenagers that everything he'd just told them was wrong. Not a bit of it was supported by Scripture. They'd become emotional about something that was completely fake.

This danger isn't new. At the end of his third missionary journey, Paul was headed back to Jerusalem. On the way he stopped and met with the elders of the Ephesian church. He gave a farewell speech and warned the Ephesians to beware those who preach false teachings about God. Paul wouldn't be around to protect them anymore, so they had to learn to protect themselves.

We must also be on guard against false teaching. As you continue to mature in your Christian faith, you'll probably encounter false teachers. Unless you test the teaching against Scripture, you'll find you're like that youth group: Looking spiritual but having no substance.

This week we'll learn that if we're going to stay healthy, then we have to defend our doctrine (our core set of beliefs). God wants us to be passionate about him, but he also wants us to be wise.

DAILY DEVOTIONS

Day 1
Acts 20:17-38

Here's the heart of a true shepherd. Paul had always protected those in his church from the destructive influences all around them. In this passage he reminds them that demonic forces must be rebuked and that false teachers will try to sneak in through the back door. Since Paul wouldn't be there to fight them off anymore, he challenged the believers to be alert. False teachers are a tough problem because they don't usually look like bad people; in fact they might seem more spiritual than most. But when they subtly begin pushing us to focus on something other than Christ, their true motives can be seen.

Have you ever thought about why you listen to certain people? Are they biblically correct in what they teach?

What standard can you use to determine if they're true teachers or not?

Ask God to provide you with righteous teachers who will steer you straight.

Day 2
2 Timothy 4:1-5

Everyone likes to be told they're right; it's flattering, and it makes us feel smart. On the other hand, people don't like to be told they're wrong; it makes them feel awkward and uncomfortable. This has always been true, even for members of the early Church.

Sometimes God will use people to tell us things that are hard to hear—things that cause us to recognize we're not acting as we should. Instead of running from such teaching (or dismissing it as wrong), we need to be open to it. If we don't, then we'll leave ourselves vulnerable to false teachers who tell us exactly what we want to hear. No one is right 100 percent of the time (not even you), so never assume you don't need someone to challenge you now and then.

How do you respond when you hear difficult things that convict you?

Ask God to show you if you have the same problem these church people did.

Day 3
Revelation 2:1-7

We don't know exactly what the Nicolaitans believed, but it was obviously a false teaching. God commended the Ephesians for testing their teachers. Instead of blindly believing everything they heard, they checked to see if what was being taught was in accordance with

Scripture. If it wasn't, then they refused to listen. We should trust those God puts in authority over us, but God's Word is the authority over all. What someone says may sound good, but we have to be sure we're trusting the Word of God, not just the words of humans. Of course in order to do that, we need to know what the Word says.

Are you studying the Word so you'd be able to spot even a minor false teaching if you heard it?

Day 4
1 John 2:18-27

John had a problem. People in his church were teaching that Jesus was never really flesh and blood—he just appeared to be. But John had known Jesus and even touched him, so he wrote this letter to clear up any confusion. You may be asking yourself, *How will I know what's right or not—don't these teachers know more than I do? How could I tell them they're wrong?* Good questions. Here John reminds his people that even though he's absent from them, the Holy Spirit is still present. This applies to us as well. The Spirit resides in us and will help us understand what's right and what isn't. That being the case, we need to make sure we're walking in step with the Holy Spirit so we'll know when false teaching appears. You don't have to be a scholar to know the real truth—just a Bible-reading, Bible-believing teenager.

Are you walking in step with the Spirit? How do you know?

Spend some time thinking through what John said. Do you really believe the Holy Spirit will teach you today?

Day 5
Acts 5:17-33

The ruling Jews were furious with the disciples for talking about Jesus. They tried silencing them time and time again. We live in a much different time today, but we can feel the same way when people in our culture tell us *not* to talk about Jesus. Very few in our society want to hear that Jesus is the only way to heaven or that they need to be saved from their sins. These are very unpopular ideas. And the moment you talk openly about these things you may get a reaction similar to the one the disciples received. We can't back down just because people want an inoffensive, watered-down faith. That kind of faith won't save anyone. We should never be ashamed of the gospel.

Do you know the truth well enough to speak openly about it, or do you keep it to yourself? Why?

Ask God to train you so that you can be as bold as the disciples were.

WEEK 41
ONE IN CHRIST: LETTER TO THE EPHESIANS (PART 1 OF 2)

MEMORY VERSE

"Consequently, you are no longer foreigners and aliens, but fellow citizens with God's people and members of God's household." (Ephesians 2:19)

INTRODUCTION

Have you ever wondered how you ended up in your family? I've wondered that about my family. I'm completely different from my parents, and I'm also fairly different from my brother. So how did we all get thrown together? We do have one major thing in common: Our last name. Whether we like it or not, we're all in the same family. And as different as we are, we have the same blood linking us.

The same is true for the Church. The New Testament church was made up of an assortment of very different kinds of people who had previously lived separate lives. What could possibly connect all these people? They now had the same bloodline—the blood of Jesus. Because of Jesus' sacrificial death, everyone who places their faith in Christ—regardless of their race, gender, or cultural background—is a part of the Church.

When Jesus rose from the dead, he began to build his family—the Church. And it was composed of people he loved and who loved him. But the members of his family would also love each other. While imprisoned in Rome, Paul wrote a letter to the church in Ephesus to help them understand their common lineage in Christ. Through this letter Paul tried to help the Ephesians see that all people are welcomed into the church family regardless of their differences.

This also holds true for your church. Wildly different people are all included—men and women, rich and poor, popular and unpopular. This week we'll look at who makes up the Church—your church—and how to live in it.

DAILY DEVOTIONS

Day 1
Ephesians 2:11-22

I grew up in the South during a time when it seemed as though just about everyone was a Christian. So I've always felt comfortable in church. Consequently, it's hard for me to imagine being far away from God since I've heard about him all my life. But here Paul reminds us that no matter how familiar we are with God or how long we've known God, we used to be far away from God. Literally, we were like aliens—strangers. Until the moment we're saved, we're completely cut off from God. That's why this is such a great passage. Now we're in! Even though we don't deserve to be a part of the Church, through Jesus we can be.

Take some time and think about what it would be like if you didn't know Jesus.

Then spend some more time thanking him for making you a part of his family.

Day 2
Ephesians 2:17-22

I know, I know—same passage as yesterday. But there's always more to find in a passage if we'll spend enough time with it. Look at the phrase "in him." It shows up twice in verses 21 and 22. Paul is telling us about the foundation of the Church. He's showing us that we aren't just a club or a group of people who happen to like being moral and singing on Sundays. He reminds us that the core of who we are is the person of Jesus. Our lives are a temple in which Jesus lives. Everything we believe should be based on him. If it's not about Jesus, then it's not really a church. But also note that you're mentioned in this verse. Verse 22 says that you, too, are a part of this building program. You're an active part of this Church that's been growing for more than 2,000 years.

Why do you go to church?

Would your life be different if you didn't go? How?

Ask God to show you how he can be the foundation of your life.

Day 3
1 Corinthians 12:14-31

We talked about this concept back in Week 11, but some principles can't be repeated enough. As you know, there are hundreds of parts in our bodies. In fact there are so many I don't even know most of them. But I'm glad to have them all, and I'd rather not lose any. Each one has a particular function and is necessary for the whole body to work properly. The same thing is true in the Church. Growing up, I used to believe the only real jobs in a church were pastor, youth minister, and music minister. But everyone—yes, even you—has a place, not just the people on the church staff. God has made you to be a vital part of your church. You have gifts that no one else has, and God wants to use you as an active, unique part of that church body.

What's your role in your church?

What are some places in your church where you can be actively involved?

Day 4
Ephesians 3:1-4

You've probably been on some sort of team. And chances are you didn't always get along with all your teammates. But they were still your teammates. If you were on a football team, then the other players were your teammates because they also played football. If you were on a drama team, then the other actors were your teammates because they also performed drama. There's always some unifying base on which a team is built. The same thing is true with the Church. For Christians the trait we all have in common is our relationship to Jesus. No matter how different we are, all Christians are our brothers and sisters. This means we can't exclude or ignore them just because they don't go to our church, and we can't shun them just because they're not our favorite people. We're on the same team with them—the Church of Jesus Christ.

Do you ever exclude some believers because they aren't like you?

What are some ways you could reach out to them instead?

Day 5
Romans 10:12-13

The Birmingham Civil Rights Institute chronicles the battle for racial equality waged on the streets of that city. That same kind of racism existed between the Jews and Gentiles. But Jesus broke down the barriers between them. The Bible is filled with verses reminding us that God shows no favoritism. Even more, no matter how different we seem to be from one another, there's one thing we all have in common—our sin. Everyone needs Jesus—everyone. So there's never a time when prejudice is justified. We all have a common problem, and we all have a common Savior. Are we ready and willing to accept everyone into the Church? Jesus is ready; and because he is, we must be, too.

Think back on how and when you became a Christian. Thank God for not excluding you.

Ask Christ to help you not exclude others, especially those who are different from you.

WEEK 42
EQUIPPING FOR MINISTRY: LETTER TO THE EPHESIANS (PART 2 OF 2)

MEMORY VERSE

"Instead, speaking the truth in love, we will in all things grow up into him who is the Head, that is, Christ." (Ephesians 4:15)

INTRODUCTION

I didn't enjoy a particular high school English class. My teacher always made me revise my essays. She was never satisfied with my first tries, and she rarely gave out compliments. Ugh! I don't even like thinking about it. But looking back years later, I now have to say that it was probably one of the best classes I ever had, and she turned out to be one of the best teachers I ever had. Why? Because she actually challenged me to learn something—and I did. In fact, I learned a lot.

Teachers aren't there to be our buddies but to make sure we learn things we may not even want to learn. Without them, we'd never become the people God wants us to be.

Still writing from prison, Paul tried to help the Ephesians understand the different kinds of leadership in the church. He was helping them see that certain people were called to teach them and to lead them. If they were going to grow in faith, then they'd have to follow these people and work toward growing as Christians.

We tend to view learning from our church leaders in the same way I viewed learning from my English teacher: "Do I have to do this?" How many sermons have we dutifully sat through without actually learning anything? But if we submit to doing the work, then we'll find we can accomplish more than before. This week we're going to look at how our pastors and teachers help equip us for life.

DAILY DEVOTIONS

Day 1
Ephesians 4:11-16

Have you ever thought that in order for people to become Christians, they should have to show up at church? It makes sense, doesn't it? I mean, the pastor can explain it so much better than we can, right? This kind of thinking can get us into trouble. According to this passage, God has given you pastors and teachers to prepare you to go share the gospel, not just bring people to church. A pastor's job is to teach you; your job is to use that training out in the real world. If we accept this fact, then church becomes our training ground—our home base from which we learn and grow—so we can fight the battles out in the world.

Do you expect the ministers in your church to do all the serious spiritual work? Is that a biblical idea?

How would your experience be different if you saw church as a training ground and its ministers as your teachers and equippers?

Day 2
Ephesians 4:11-16

It's time for a reality check. Do you really want to grow spiritually? Honestly? Everyone needs to grow up spiritually, but this doesn't happen automatically. You can show up at church for the next 10 years and not grow one bit unless you choose to do so. But if you really do want to grow, then ask yourself how you're accomplishing that goal—or how you can start to do so. You may already be doing the right things but not really putting any effort into it; you know, going through the motions. Or there may be things you need to change. Get honest about whether you really want to grow spiritually because no one can help you grow if you don't want to.

Spend some time asking yourself this question: Do I really want to grow?

In your prayer time today, ask God to give you a real desire to grow and show you ways to do so.

Day 3
1 Peter 3:15-16

This has always been one of those extra-challenging Scripture passages for me. If you've ever gotten into a spiritual debate that's way over your head, then you know how hard defending your faith can be. The thing to remember is that everyone starts somewhere. And no one expects you to have all the answers. (I certainly don't have them all.) But you should be able to hold your own about your beliefs. Instead of saying, "Let's go ask my pastor," you need to be able to explain to others why you're a Christian and why you believe what you do. This requires some hard work, since you have to stop and think about what you believe. Have you ever done that?

Spend some time thinking about what you believe.

Ask God to help you understand your relationship with him.

Day 4
Galatians 1:13-24

Did you catch verse 18? Three years! After Paul got saved, he didn't just take off on his first missionary journey. Even though he was one of the smartest Jews around, he still needed to be trained and that wasn't a quick process. He spent three years learning about Christ before he went to teach anyone anything. If Paul needed that kind of training, then we do as well. After you become a Christian, there's a lot to learn, and you won't learn it overnight. So cut yourself some slack; you're not supposed to understand everything yet. We should all get to work. We have a lot to learn, and we need to be as diligent about learning as Paul was.

Are you putting yourself in places where you can learn from those who've been walking with Jesus longer than you have? If not, then what's your reason for not doing so?

Pray for God to help you grow by learning what he wants you to learn today.

Day 5
Luke 10:1-23

"Aren't you coming with us?" I bet that was the first thing on these guys' minds when Jesus sent them out. They'd been following Jesus and watching him do miracles, but now Jesus was sending them out on a solo flight. And that's very different. Being equipped isn't just sitting and listening; it's experiencing ministry. Part of your training will actually be witnessing to someone, going on short-term mission trips, and serving in your church. You may not feel ready yet, but no one ever feels really ready. Be willing to take the opportunities God throws your way so you can continue growing.

Do you avoid any situation in which you aren't perfectly comfortable?

Could you be missing out on something God is asking you to experience?

Look for a ministry opportunity that God may be asking you to try today. Then do it—even if you don't feel completely comfortable yet. Ask God to give you courage and teach you something new through the experience. You have to stretch in order to grow.

WEEK 43
TESTIMONY IN CHAINS: PAUL'S ARREST

MEMORY VERSE

"Paul replied, 'Short time or long—I pray God that not only you but all who are listening to me today may become what I am, except for these chains.'" (Acts 26:29)

INTRODUCTION

Joni Eareckson Tada has one of those stories that just amazes. After a diving accident left her a quadriplegic at age 17, Joni found herself facing a life much different than the one she thought she was going to live. Yet her disability wasn't strong enough to keep her from serving Christ. She's written more than 30 books and traveled to more than 40 countries. She's also a sought-after speaker, as well as an advocate for the disabled. It probably wasn't the life Joni had in mind when she a teenager, but her ministry has reached millions.

When we find ourselves in difficult circumstances that force us to change our plans, we have two choices. We can either choose to give up, or we can choose to continue to serve Christ—no matter what.

When faced with a particularly difficult time, the apostle Paul chose to serve Christ. In Acts 24 through 26, we find the story of Paul's imprisonment and trials. Paul could have given up at any point—he faced some pretty tough circumstances. But he stayed true to his calling and continued to preach the message of Jesus Christ. Paul couldn't see the future, but he knew God had plans for him—even in jail. How would you have responded?

This week we're going to face one of the hardest questions of life: How do we serve God when things don't go our way?

DAILY DEVOTIONS

Day 1
Acts 24:24-27; 25:9-12; 26:24-32

So what do you do if you're Paul and you find yourself in jail for more than two years? Pout? Sulk? Get angry? Paul may have had days when he did all of these things; but for the most part, we know what he did while in prison. It was the same thing he did before he was arrested— he preached about Jesus. Paul had been called to spread the name of Jesus. So no matter where he found himself, he continued doing just that. When things don't go as we plan, or we don't get to serve the way we want, it's easy to throw in the towel. But then we miss out on all of God's unexpected blessings.

Prison couldn't stop Paul. Are you letting anything stop you?

If your life's dreams never come true, will you still serve Christ as best you can?

Spend some time today praying about anything that's hindering you from serving Christ with everything you have.

Day 2
Philippians 1:12-18

Paul appeared to be an optimist. He wasn't getting to do what he wanted. (I'm sure he would've rather been planting churches or preaching in a marketplace.) Instead, he was in prison, and it didn't look like he'd be getting out anytime soon. But Paul saw the bigger picture: Even his imprisonment was advancing the gospel. Paul wrote the letters of Philippians, Colossians, Ephesians, and Philemon from jail. And these letters have helped believers for almost 2,000 years. I'm sure letter writing wasn't his favorite form of ministry, but God used it. Even when life doesn't go the way you want, God can use you greatly.

If God gave you a plan that was different than the one you wanted, would you follow it anyway?

Think about some things in your past that you didn't enjoy. Ask God to show you how these events were used for good in your life—or someone else's.

Day 3
Hebrews 11:32-39

When bad things happen, sometimes I wonder, *Did I do something wrong? Is God punishing me?* Satan will tell us "yes," whether it's true or not. When we face setbacks in our plans, we may wonder if we really have God's blessing. But look at today's passage. While God blessed many people in the Old Testament, the list changes course mid-verse (v. 35) and talks of others who had a rougher time. But all of them are commended, regardless of their circumstances. Just because you're struggling in your attempts to serve, that doesn't mean God has forgotten you. Don't look at your circumstances to determine whether God is with you; rely on God's Word.

Do you find security in your circumstances—or in God's Word? (Think back to your last crisis to find out.)

Ask God to give you strength to endure when things seem confusing.

Day 4
Psalm 42

The Bible is nothing if not honest. Some may picture the saints of old as perfect men who calmly endured affliction; but the Scriptures reveal otherwise. The psalms typically show the raw emotions of people walking through tough times. Today's psalmist declared he'd still hope in God even though the reasons he once had been joyful had all collapsed. Why was he so confident? Because even though his circumstances had changed, his God had not. The God he worshiped when things were good is the God he'd continue to worship even though life was now hard. This kind of worship requires a choice to believe despite our feelings. The results might surprise you: This woeful writer found not only comfort from God, but also a chance to encourage people like us thousands of years later.

Think about a time when you chose to worship even when you didn't feel like it.

Write your own psalm to God today below. Above all, be honest with God.

Day 5
Acts 24:24-27

Okay, let's say you're Paul. You know you're supposed to be out spreading the Word of God; but you're stuck in jail, and the guy holding you prisoner obviously wants a bribe. You could easily get your hands on the money, since you have a lot of friends who want to get you out. What do you do? I'm sure Paul could have found a way to bribe Felix, yet he stayed put for two years. Why? Because the ends didn't justify the means. God is in control, and God won't ask us to violate our faith even if we have a logical reason for doing so. God hasn't forgotten. You'll get taken care of no matter what your circumstances. Be patient. Even though you may not understand what's going on, God does. Your job is to continue to trust him.

Have you ever rationalized a sin because you thought you had a good reason? If so, describe why that was the wrong thing to do.

Decide to react in a godly manner instead of a selfish manner when it comes to making tough decisions.

WEEK 44
AN INDIRECT PATH: PAUL SAILS FOR ROME

MEMORY VERSE

"But the centurion wanted to spare Paul's life and kept them from carrying out their plan. He ordered those who could swim to jump overboard first and get to land." (Acts 27:43)

INTRODUCTION

Carnivals are fun. As a kid I looked forward to going to the carnival every year because I'd get to ride the Scrambler. Have you ever ridden the Scrambler? It flings you left and right, back and forth, all while moving in a huge circle. It was fun...unless you'd eaten a funnel cake right before you got on.

Often our Christian journey resembles the Scrambler. You expect it to be a calm journey that moves predictably from one stage to the next. But what you actually get is a sudden move to the left, then to the right, then forward, then backward.

In Acts 27:27–28:6 Paul went through a journey sort of like this. Amazingly, he endures a huge storm, a shipwreck, and a snake attack. Paul thought Rome would be his big obstacle, only to find that his journey to get there would be just as eventful. But God was in control, and God is in control even when we can't discern the reasons for our trouble. Our job is to stick close to God, hold on tight, and trust him even though we don't always understand where we're going.

Through it all, we can serve Christ along the way. So get ready, your Christian journey might be a lot more exciting than you thought. Oh, and you might want to skip that funnel cake.

DAILY DEVOTIONS

Day 1
Acts 27:27–28:6

Who says the Bible isn't exciting? One thing is sure: Following God is a greater adventure than anything else we might do. So if we're bored, it's not God's fault. Paul probably wasn't expecting all this to happen when he chose to go to Rome, but here again we see him serving God wherever he is. All the men on the ship respect Paul's decisions even though he's one of the prisoners, and he ends up witnessing to the locals and the governor. These things may not have been on the itinerary, but Paul made the most of his circumstances. Our lives don't always go according to our plans, either, but we can still make the most of every opportunity. We just have to choose to do so.

How can you make the most of your opportunities today?

Spend some time praying that God would prepare you for whatever lies ahead.

Day 2
1 Samuel 17:32-37

This passage is part of the infamous David and Goliath incident. (If you've never read the entire story, then read chapter 17.) Here's the background: David had been anointed king over Israel, but he'd been tending sheep for years. And he wouldn't get to be king for a few years more as God was using this time to prepare David. Now to today's passage: David said he wasn't afraid of Goliath because of two prior incidents, one with a bear and one with a lion. Imagine being David. He was supposed to be king, and he ended up fighting a bear. *What does this have to do with being king?* he may have wondered. Well, on this particular day David found out. Even when your life seems to make no sense at all, trust that God is doing things we won't understand until later—if ever.

What does this story tell you about God?

Decide to trust God regardless of how your circumstances appear.

Day 3
Exodus 13:20-22; 40:34-38

If you were an Israelite during the exodus and you ever wondered whether God was with you, then you could just take a look at the tabernacle. The Israelites could actually see God's presence day or night as it covered the tabernacle. You may wish God would do that today. Wouldn't that make it easier to know God's always with us? True, but remember that even though they could see the presence of God with them, he led them in a way they didn't understand at all. To them it looked as though that cloud was leading them on a wild goose chase through the desert. But the point was to teach them to follow God, no matter what. God is trying to teach us the same thing. Instead of following a cloud, we get to follow the Spirit. Sometimes the route will seem odd, but our call is still the same: "Follow me."

Try to put yourself in the Israelites' shoes. After 27 years would you find it easy or hard to keep following God? Why?

Ask God to lead you by his Spirit today. Commit to follow the Holy Spirit no matter what.

Day 4
Acts 28:1-6

Some people believe that if you're spiritual, then you can pick up poisonous snakes—and even get bitten by one—yet not be killed. (Yes, this is one of the passages they cite to prove it.) But that's not really the point here. Paul didn't go out of his way to find a snake to play with. God had his hand on Paul and used this incident to open a door for sharing the gospel. Paul now had a chance to tell the people that he wasn't a god but he knew the real One. God doesn't create miracles for everyone, but his purposes remain unchanged. You don't need snakes to prove you're holy; you can prove that by staying true to God's purposes and living according to God's plans.

Have you ever seen someone take Scripture and use it out of context (like using this passage to mean that if we're super spiritual, then poisonous snakes won't affect us)?

Day 5

2 Corinthians 11:21-33

Paul's life and writings shaped Western civilization as we know it. Of course God was in charge of that, and without Christ Paul wouldn't have amounted to much. But let's not forget Satan in all of this. We have an enemy who seeks to destroy us every day, and the list of hardships in this passage indicates that those of us who want to serve Christ wholeheartedly will have a fight on our hands. Remember: Satan doesn't win when we follow Christ—no matter what happens! It might be painful, difficult, dangerous, and trying, but our circumstances cannot stop us if we truly rely on God. Paul's life is a testimony to that fact. Are you letting your circumstances stop you from being like Paul?

What do we learn about God's wisdom and control through this passage?

Ask God to use you as he used Paul, regardless of the path you must take.

WEEK 45
EVERY OPPORTUNITY: PAUL PREACHES IN PRISON

MEMORY VERSE

"Therefore I want you to know that God's salvation has been sent to the Gentiles, and they will listen!" (Acts 28:28)

INTRODUCTION

God uses us in amazing ways, and many times we don't even see it coming. A few years ago I was preaching at a summer camp on a college campus. One night I went backstage to help counsel the students who responded to the invitation to become Christians. But I stopped in the restroom on the way. As I entered the bathroom, a young guy followed me. After a few awkward pleasantries, he said, "I've never really been saved before." He told me this in the bathroom. (I definitely didn't see that one coming!) So, after we walked *out* of the restroom, I had the privilege of introducing him to Christ.

When we left Paul last week, he was just getting to Rome. In Acts 28 we find out that, just as before, Paul was going to be in jail for a long time. For some people this would've been a huge letdown. But for Paul? No problem. He didn't allow pesky details like imprisonment keep him from faithfully sharing the gospel every day.

Opportunities to serve and share Christ are everywhere. The trick is learning to see them. Once we realize that we can literally serve Christ 24/7, things get interesting. This week we're going to try to follow Paul's lead and learn how to take advantage of every opportunity we find to serve Christ.

DAILY DEVOTIONS

Day 1
Acts 28:16-31

How's this for dedication? Paul was under house arrest while awaiting his trial, and he couldn't go out of his house to tell others about Jesus. I might have given up at this point—or at least felt sorry for myself. But Paul didn't have time for sulking. This was just another obstacle with a God-sized solution: If Paul can't go to the people, then get the people to come to Paul! Sometimes we won't get the opportunities to serve God that we'd like, but opportunities are around us nonetheless. Paul decided to serve no matter what the circumstances. Therefore, he had a huge impact for God's kingdom. When we decide to use every circumstance, we'll also see God moving in great ways.

Think about some creative ways to share Christ during the activities you'll be involved in today.

Ask God to give you the kind of dedication that drove Paul to use every opportunity for Christ.

Day 2
Ephesians 5:15-17

We should never forget that we have an enemy who wants us to waste opportunities. Verse 16 reminds us that the days in which we live are evil. Most of the time we skip over phrases like this. But a spiritual war is really going on, and you're involved whether you like it or not. As we have opportunities to share the gospel, to serve, and to love others, we'll also experience temptation to ignore those opportunities. We must recognize that this temptation is a spiritual attack. If you expect to be tempted, then you'll be better prepared to fight off those enemy attacks.

What temptations does Satan use the most in your life to keep you from serving Christ?

How can you best defend yourself against those temptations?

Go back to Ephesians 6:10-18 and pray through your spiritual armor today.

Day 3
Hebrews 3:12-15

I believe procrastination is something everyone wrestles with. If an assignment is due Friday, then we can wait until at least...Thursday night, right? The problem with procrastinating spiritually is that some opportunities come along only once. The writer of Hebrews knew this and urged his readers to do what God asked them to do immediately—not next Friday. If we procrastinate, then we may lose out on the opportunity forever. We may also lose spiritual ground as sin sinks deeper into our daily routine. We have to be relentless about taking opportunities when they arise because we're not guaranteed to ever have them again. This even applies to talking to your best friend about Jesus. You may never get another chance. Use the one you have!

What spiritual opportunity have you missed because of procrastination?

How can you prepare yourself to seize opportunities today?

Day 4
Philippians 3:12-13

Most of us feel more guilt about the opportunities we've wasted than joy about the ones we've seized. How do we turn things around and put ourselves in the joy column? When we rely on ourselves to go out and serve, we can only do so much. Paul relied on God's power instead of his own; that way, no matter where he found himself, Paul knew he was right where God wanted him. God isn't sending you on a solo mission; God wants you to lean on him. Don't view today as a test, but as a joint mission. Let God empower you and see what happens.

Think back to the last thing you did for God. Whose power did you rely on? What were the results?

Ask God to help you rely on him instead of yourself.

Day 5
Acts 28:30-31

Kind of an odd way to end a book, isn't it? Luke leaves us with this picture of Paul preaching while still under house arrest in Rome. But this wasn't the end for Paul. We know he ultimately got out of jail and continued to travel and preach the gospel before he was ultimately rearrested, retried, and executed for his faith. Why end it this way? God is the main character in this story, not Paul or Peter. So it's fitting that Luke finished his book with an image of Paul faithfully spreading the gospel despite his imprisonment. God fulfilled his promise to bring Paul to Rome, and God continued to use Paul. As we've seen throughout the book of Acts, nothing can stop the advance of the gospel.

What have you learned about God through the book of Acts?

Spend some time reflecting on the whole book and write about what stands out the most.

WEEK 46
YOUR ROLE: PETER AND THE PRIESTHOOD OF BELIEVERS

MEMORY VERSE

"But you are a chosen people, a royal priesthood, a holy nation, a people belonging to God, that you may declare the praises of him who called you out of darkness into his wonderful light." (1 Peter 2:9)

INTRODUCTION

I don't know how your family does it, but in order to accommodate all the people at my family's Thanksgiving, we had a kiddie table for anyone under 18. I never liked the kiddie table. I felt I was missing out on everything just because I wasn't old enough. All I wanted was to be a big person.

I'm sure the Old Testament Jews also felt this way since almost none of them were allowed in the Temple. It wasn't that they weren't old enough; they weren't holy enough. Only the priests could go before God.

This week we're going to consider an important Christian belief called "the priesthood of the believer." It means that when you become a Christian, you become a priest of sorts. Instead of there being only a few priests who go before God for us, as believers in Jesus we all get full access to God. In the early Church, Peter was the one everyone looked to for spiritual guidance. But he was adamant about helping people understand that he wasn't the only one who could communicate with God. We all can listen and talk to God through Jesus Christ. Together we're all a "holy priesthood."

As a Christian you also have complete access to all the blessings in Christ because he's forgiven you and adopted you. You don't need a middleman to go to God on your behalf. But it goes even further than that. Because you have this access, God wants to use you like a priest, one who helps other people find God. It sounds like a big task but don't worry. Christ will help you every step of the way.

DAILY DEVOTIONS

Day 1
1 Peter 2:4-10

When I think about my church, I typically focus on the building. But Peter explains that *we're* the building. All of us are living parts of God's temple—designed to be the place where God is experienced and worshiped. In the Old Testament, priests lived in the temple, but now every believer is a priest who takes the presence of God with her wherever she goes. So instead of trying to get everyone into a physical temple, God is building a living temple that will literally encompass every Christian—everywhere.

How does it change your idea of the Christian life to realize that God wants to use you as a priest?

Ask God to help you understand what it means for you to serve as a priest today.

Day 2
1 John 5:13-15

I've often wondered if God hears my prayers. However, the Bible is clear about the answer. In the Old Testament, people went to the temple to give offerings and to worship God. Priests were the mediators between the people and God. Then Christ changed everything. John was confident in this passage saying God hears our prayers because we're believers. You don't need a priest; you have direct access to God through the Holy Spirit. We now have the privilege that previously only the priests had. That being said, we should be in tune with the Spirit as we pray, asking for things God would approve of, not just things we selfishly want. The Old Testament priests did this, and we must do it as well. Rest assured, your prayers are heard.

When you pray, do you seek to be in line with God's will, or do you just ask for whatever you want?

Thank God for giving us access to him in a way many others before us never experienced.

Day 3
James 5:16

Since we're talking about being priests, let's look at this verse again. Does it make more sense to you now than it did back in Week 8 of our study? It's important that we confess our sins to each other, as well as to God, because we're all priests. Each one of us can become the vehicle through which God provides blessings and help. If we never confess to one another, then we ignore the fact that God is working through all of us. It also means that, as a priest, I can ask Jesus to pour his love through me to someone else. Sometimes we wish Jesus were here physically so we could talk to him, hold on to him, and lean on him. James reminds us that these things will happen when we live as priests of the Holy God.

Who are the Christians with whom you can be completely honest?

Ask Christ to use you to share his love with someone today.

Day 4
1 Timothy 2:1-8

Have you ever thought God probably listens to the prayers of really spiritual people, but not those of ordinary people? This week we're learning that ordinary people don't exist. We're all important because we're all part of the holy nation of God. Because of this, Paul knew the prayers of the Church are incredibly powerful. Never underestimate your place in God's kingdom. Because you're a child of God, you have the privilege of interceding on behalf of other people. Your prayers can bring great change in the lives of your friends and family. Try it and see.

Do you pray as if your prayers will have an impact, or do you pray as if no one really listens to you? Why?

Spend some time praying for your friends and family. Pray knowing who you are in Christ.

Day 5
Psalm 84

You may have sung the praise song "Better Is One Day" in your church before. In case you didn't know, the song came from this psalm. The psalmist is thinking about being in God's presence, and he loves it. In his mind just being a doorkeeper for God would be better than being anywhere else for thousands of years. The great thing for us is that this is a reality. It's not just the chosen few who'll get to live in God's presence forever, but anyone who believes in the name of Jesus. God wants you to be in his presence, and because you know God, you're invited to live with God forever. Once upon a time, it was only the priests who could get anywhere near God. But now that privilege extends to the entire house of God—including you.

What would it be like to live in God's presence every day?

Do you really believe God wants you to be that close to him? Believe it because God does!

WEEK 47
THE CHURCH PREPARED: JOHN'S VISION

MEMORY VERSE

"Therefore, since we are surrounded by such a great cloud of witnesses, let us throw off everything that hinders and the sin that so easily entangles, and let us run with perseverance the race marked out for us." (Hebrews 12:1)

INTRODUCTION

Have you ever seen a dead church? It's kind of depressing. I know of one. It's small, and the cemetery next to it is the only part that still gets visitors. Through an open doorway, you can see the pews and the place where the pulpit used to be. Those windows might have once held stained glass, but the church is dead. No one meets there anymore, and who knows what happened to the people. It's a sad commentary, but it ought to remind us of the spiritual battle we're all involved in. It should also make us perk up and stay alert to Satan's plans to destroy us however he can.

Jesus will never abandon a church without a fight. The book of Revelation is about a vision John had while exiled on the island of Patmos. Through this vision a message was sent to seven churches, challenging and encouraging them to stand firm. The stakes were huge; they could have lost it all or gained a crown of glory.

Jesus is returning one day, and he'll do everything he can to make sure we're prepared before he comes. That means he sometimes has to tell us things that are hard to hear, but it's for our own good. And when we obey his commands, we can be confident that he'll bring about all he's promised. This week we're going to examine what Jesus said to those seven churches—and find out how we can protect our own.

DAILY DEVOTIONS

Day 1
Revelation 2:1-7

It's possible to get so caught up in what you're doing that you forget why you're doing it. This can even happen to us as believers. When we're doing a lot of spiritual things, and we forget why we're doing them, then it does us no good. Jesus is telling the church in Ephesus that keeping everyone pure is important; however, the main thing is to be in love with Jesus. It's easier to drift away from this love than we think. We can do godly things but still forget about God. How about you? Is your main focus being in a love relationship with Jesus? It's not enough to *look* spiritual; we have to *be* spiritual.

What's your first love?

If this message were for you, what would you need to repent of in order to make Jesus your first love?

Day 2
Revelation 2:8-11

If Jesus knows it's going to happen, then why doesn't he stop it? Because all is not as it seems. Smyrna may seem poor in the world's eyes, but Jesus reveals that they have treasures unlike anything this world has seen. Even when they undergo persecution, God uses their suffering for his glory and to draw people to himself. When we face harsh circumstances, we have to remember there's more going on than meets the eye. To us it may seem bad, but our future glory will far outweigh the suffering we endure here. This requires faith, for sure; but the fact that God sent this message shows that God is in control and has a plan and a future for us. We can never let our circumstances determine our faithfulness. We must decide to be faithful no matter what.

What was comforting about this letter to the church in Smyrna?

What will you have to endure to follow Christ today? Pray for yourself and for all those who will face persecution.

Day 3
Revelation 2:12-17

Can you imagine hearing God say, "Satan lives in your neighborhood"? The church in Pergamum must have had strong faith to live in that kind of environment. But even they had compromised. They'd resisted Satan in some areas, but they'd also allowed some other sins to creep into their lives. This is a common problem. When you're already standing firm on the really big issues, it's sometimes easy to fudge on the seemingly smaller matters. Why worry about swearing when you have to stand firm against premarital sex and drug use? But just because we're faithful in big areas, that doesn't mean we have the freedom to compromise. Jesus is sternly reminding Pergamum to keep alert in *all* areas.

Are there parts of your life that you've allowed to be less than what God desires?

Ask God to reveal to you any place in your life that you've compromised with sin.

Day 4
Revelation 2:18-29

You may not understand all the details of what was going on in Thyatira, but you can get the gist of it. The majority of the church was growing, but someone encouraged them to go astray into odd sexual practices and secret rituals. Everyone loves secrets, so this had apparently snagged a lot of the Thyatirans. Jesus reminds us that even Christians will be called to account for our actions. If we love Christ, then we must stay alert and avoid sin in any form.

Is there anyone in your church or school who's tempting people to do things that would dishonor Christ—even a little bit? How would you confront someone who was doing this in your church?

How would you protect yourself and others from their influence?

Pray for wisdom in facing such situations now—or in the future—if you're called to do so.

Day 5
Revelation 3:1-6

This would've been a depressing message to hear from God. Or maybe it was just the kind of wake-up call the church in Sardis needed. It makes no difference what people see on the outside. Even if people believe we have a great church and come faithfully every week, that doesn't mean we're truly alive. The goal of a church—or even your youth group—isn't to be popular but to be rooted in Christ. How can you tell which is which? Well, when you talk about your church, do you talk about how God is changing people and what God is calling you to do as a church? Or do you talk about who came, what they did, and how much fun it was—without referring to Christ at all? It could be a life-and-death question.

If Jesus never showed up at your next church meeting, would anyone notice?

WEEK 48
THE CHURCH ETERNAL: THE NEW JERUSALEM

MEMORY VERSE

"The Lord is not slow in keeping his promise, as some understand slowness. He is patient with you, not wanting anyone to perish, but everyone to come to repentance." (2 Peter 3:9)

INTRODUCTION

Harps, clouds, and white—lots of white. That's the picture most of us have when we think about heaven. To be honest, heaven has always seemed kind of gaudy to me. I mean…pearly gates and streets of gold? If this is our picture of heaven, then it's not going to be much of a motivational factor in the life of the Church. Who wants to go to a place where you have to sit in a choir loft for all eternity?

The truth is that heaven is going to be a place more magnificent than your wildest dreams. The Bible says that when Christ returns and takes us home, he's going to make everything new. All the pain and frustration we deal with now—and all the things that cause them—will be gone. Can you imagine what it will be like to not have to deal with sin anymore, to never have to wrestle with your thoughts again, to live in a place where you can see Jesus with your very own eyes?

If heaven seems boring to you, then you don't have a very clear picture of it. This week we're going to look at the eternal future of the Church. We're going to have to use our imaginations, but the Holy Spirit has given us some guidelines in Scripture to help us understand a place that's so amazing we don't even have the words to describe it.

DAILY DEVOTIONS

Day 1
Revelation 21:1-8

If we see a problem with something, then it's almost natural to want to fix it and make it better. Now imagine that happening on a global scale. When Jesus returns, everything is going to be changed; he's going to make everything new. How do you improve on a sunset? Or a galaxy? The big improvement will be that God will eradicate sin once and for all, and we'll be able to live with him as we were intended to. But God isn't going to simply patch up the old world; he's going to fix it once and for all.

Let's try an exercise. God gave you an imagination for a reason—now use it to picture what the new world might be like. Then remember that nothing we can dream up will even come close to what God has in store for us. Buckle up; it's coming soon!

Day 2
1 Corinthians 15:35-49

We don't talk about this enough. Most of us know that our souls will go to be with Jesus when we die, but we often forget that Jesus promised us a bodily resurrection. Jesus was raised body and soul from the dead, and so will we be—body and soul. How will that work? Well, no one knows for sure, but Paul reminds us that it will happen. We're going to have some sort of physical body that's completely spiritual; one that will never wear out, get old, or die. It will even be glorious! We'll walk into heaven, not float. And while we won't get wings (we won't become angels), we also won't be disappointed with our new appearance.

If our bodies, as well as our souls, will be raised, then should we take better care of our current bodies?

Spend some time thinking about what a new spiritual body might be like.

Day 3
Revelation 2:17; 21:2-3

Sometimes it may seem as if God is a million miles away from us. Those are the times when we really have to live by faith—knowing that God's presence is with us even when we can't feel it. But when we go to live with God, it's going to be very different. Look at the images in these verses. God will give you a special name that will be known only to you and God. It's a special name you'll share together. Then we're described as a bride meeting her husband at the altar. It's a very intimate image. God won't be like a king leading his people from afar. God will be among us. We'll get to see God, and we'll have a relationship that's closer than anything we've ever known.

Try to imagine what it will be like to experience God in this way.

Since God wants to be as close to you as possible, even now, how can you grow closer to God today?

Day 4
Revelation 20:11-15; 21:8

Charles Spurgeon said that if you ever preach about hell, then it should be done with tears in your eyes. The bliss of heaven is rivaled only by the nightmarish reality of hell—eternal separation from God. There's no middle ground. Those who choose to reject an eternity with God are doomed to a life forever without God. Does God purposefully send people to hell? The great Christian writer C.S. Lewis has a good answer to this question: All those who are in hell choose it. In other words, they either choose to be with God or choose to be without God, and God will honor their choice—even if it is hell. But if this is the only option for those who don't know Christ, then we should be doing everything in our powers to make sure they choose wisely.

Who do you know who isn't a believer? Ask God for an opportunity to talk to that person about a relationship with Christ.

Day 5
Revelation 22:1-6

Much of the book of Revelation is symbolic, so we don't know what heaven will look like exactly. However, these passages help us understand what it will be like generally. Notice where we are: There's the Tree of Life from Genesis, but now it's not in a garden; it's in the middle of a city. What started with Adam and Eve has become a Church made up of believers from all nations. When we get there, we'll live in a community where there's no fear, no violence, no pain, no mistrust, and no oppression. No one will ever mistreat anyone else; you'll never be laughed at, ignored, left out, abused, or mistreated again. Imagine living with a group of people like that—where everyone you meet is as close and trustworthy as your best friend. Now that's a place worth waiting for!

Does your youth group or church look more like this new community than the rest of the world? Why or why not?

How can you help form that kind of community here on earth now?

A FINAL WORD

Think back on all that you've read: The Holy Spirit coming at Pentecost; the apostles' experiences with persecution, imprisonment, and beatings; the death-on-the-spot of Ananias and Sapphira; Stephen's murder; Paul's conversion, missionary journeys, shipwreck, and ultimate imprisonment in Rome; and so much more. Trying to comprehend all this information is like drinking from a fire hose—it's almost too much to swallow. But more than just a collection of great stories, there are some solid principles to be learned from each lesson.

The story of the New Testament church teaches us so much about being a member of Christ's Church. We're not designed to stand alone. As followers of Christ, we're meant to live within the body of believers, contribute our gifts and prayers to the Church, and work to spread the good news of Christ throughout the world. We're meant to put all our energies into uplifting our fellow believers, as well as those who've never heard the gospel. But remember, you're not a member of your local church only, but of the global Church, the family of Christians everywhere. These are the lessons of the New Testament church.

Hopefully you've learned these lessons after going through this book. God calls his children to a higher standard. By focusing on what Christian community is—as you've done the last 48 weeks—you've learned what it means to live the Christian life in the context of the Church and of the world. And through the power of the Holy Spirit, you have the opportunity to live the same kind of exciting, fruitful life described in the book of Acts. Allow God to take control of your life—and hold on for the ride! There's no telling what you'll experience.

Invite your students to spend 48 weeks in these life-changing devotionals. With daily scripture and thoughts, questions to get them thinking, and plenty of space for students to journal their thoughts, your teens will gain a deeper understanding and appreciation for issues that really affect their faith.

Character
Old Testament People—Encounters with God
Richard Parker
RETAIL $12.99
ISBN 978-0-310-27906-8

Christ
The Life of Christ—The Basics of Faith
Dr. Johnny Derouen
RETAIL $12.99
ISBN 978-0-310-27905-1

Community
The New Testament Church—The Essence of Fellowship
Adam Robinson
RETAIL $12.99
ISBN 978-0-310-27907-5

Many people think teenagers aren't capable of much. But Zach Hunter is proving those people wrong. He's only fifteen, but he's working to end slavery in the world—and he's making changes that affect millions of people. Find out how Zach is making a difference and how you can make changes in the things that you see wrong with our world.

Be the Change
Your Guide to Freeing Slaves and
Changing the World
Zach Hunter
RETAIL $9.99
ISBN 978-0-310-27756-9

Our world is broken, but you can change that. Zach Hunter is a teenage activist, working to end modern-day slavery and other problems facing the world. He believes your generation can be the one to change our world for the better. Inside you'll read stories of real students changing the world, and find tangible ideas you can use to be the generation of change.

Generation Change
Roll Up Your Sleeves and Change
the World
Zach Hunter
RETAIL $12.99
ISBN 978-0-310-28515-1

invert